The Magic of Consciousness Workshops

Additional works by Mr. Knape
available soon from Preparation Press:

The Magic of Consciousness series:
Workshops

Mother
(Scheduled for publication in 2006)
Daughter
(Scheduled for publication in 2006)
Father
(Scheduled for publication in 2007)
Son
(Scheduled for publication in 2007)

The Guardian Chronicles series:
The Knight of the Temple, Vol. 1
(Scheduled for publication in 2006)

Further information on these and other works
is available at: www.preparationpress.com

The Magic of Consciousness Workshops

By Glen Knape

Preparation Press
Whittier, CA

The Magic of Consciousness – Workshops

by Glen Knape

Second edition, 2005

Preparing the way

Preparation Press
Whittier, CA, USA
www.preparationpress.com

Cover Art: "D.K. Vista 2", by Lucette Bourdin,
http://www.lbourdin.com/

ISBN 0-9760084-1-6

Disclaimer

This is a work of nonfiction, structured as a dialogue.

All of the characters included herein are entirely fictional. They represent archetypes, not real persons, and any resemblance between them and real persons, living or deceased, is purely coincidental. The opinions expressed by these characters do not represent those of the author, the publisher, or anyone else. The location of the classes, and the classes themselves, are also wholly imaginary. No such location exists and no such classes occurred. They are all, simply and entirely, a means of posing ideas, asking and answering questions, and taking the reader through a series of inner experiences.

However, the ideas and inner experiences at the heart of the text, around which the characters, setting, and classes revolve, are entirely real.

Editor's Foreword

The Magic of Consciousness – Workshops is part of a series of dialogues featuring Ellora Porter and her father Quinn MacAndrews. Its purpose is to explain the work of the Ashram of Synthesis. It is set in an imaginary spiritual center at which Quinn is leading a series of four workshops. Most of those attending the workshops have quite a different perspective than Quinn, which creates the potential for considerable disagreement.

At the time this work begins, Ellora is barely beginning to recover from a series of traumatic adventures which ended when she found her father, Quinn. Quinn is the first person to recognize Ellora's potential and, in addition to helping her recover, is helping her find her self and use her abilities. Those abilities include highly sensitive clairvoyance and clairaudience, and thus Ellora's function in these works is to observe and comment on what she sees.

This work is set during a period of transition, when some of the outer expressions of the Synthesis Ashram were struggling to understand each other, and the dialogue reflects this.

The Magic of Consciousness – Workshops was written for experienced, knowledgeable esotericists. The 'First Edition' was released at the 2005 Seven Ray Institute conference, and was slightly revised for this second edition.

Table of Contents

Dramatis Personae

Amanda Flintwright – "retired" disciple
Over fifty years practicing the Ageless Wisdom —
Bailey books and Arcane School, plus a great deal more.

Reed-thin, frail looking, but alert and cheerful, her
aura is a clear, blazing blue, almost white at the crown
and darkening to bright indigo further down.

Angelique Laroche – Teaching Petal of Wisdom
Group Heart Center Took N.S. and T.T. in 1990s.
Has taught N.S. and is teaching a second time.

Function within Synthesis Ashram to help project
the Wisdom to humanity.

Arista Jaspar – White Magician (ritualist)
Arcane School throughout the '80s. Has explored a
number of forms of ritual magic, and is developing her
own order, but nothing "feels" right.

Radiant indigo around heart center, with forest
green at the throat, blending into something like tur-
quoise in the ajna. Classic "Rubenesque" figure.

Celine Garner – Synthesis/Cave Center
Theosophy, Bailey, *Nature of the Soul* and *Teacher
Training*. Esoteric Astrologer, Co-Mason. Part of the
nucleus of the Wisdom Group Cave Center.

As thin as one of Brian Froud's faeries, with indigo-
white cascading into the top of her head, flowing into
central blue-white point, and out through her brow.

Chantel – Synthesis Deva
Part of the new order of Synthesis Devas. Is charged
with guarding and guiding Ellora. Primarily Indigo in
color, with radiant violet "wings" fountaining up from
her heart. Particularly helpful in scouting, teaching
Ellora how to interpret etheric sounds and colors and to

interact with Devas and elementals, warning about dangers, and insulating Ellora from harmful energies and forces.

Ellee Kyoushi – Educator
Studied "Education in the New Age" particularly closely and is participating in efforts to formulate a new educational system. Place on Soul levels within the Teaching Group of the Synthesis Ashram. Early thirties.

Ellora Porter (Me) – Quinn's daughter
A twelve-year-old girl. Very sensitive clairvoyance and clairaudience. A musician (harpist). Place and function is within a Group Unit responsible for sounding the note of Synthesis within the planetary life. More specifically, she is part of a petal of its group throat center that is responsible for expressing synthetic sound within inner and outer ritual – that Sound which Orders Chaos.

Halifax Kelley (Hal) – Esoteric Psychologist
Extensive knowledge of Bailey. Studied psychosynthesis at the Psychosynthesis Institute. Professional counselor.

Hugh Connelly – Throat Center of Wisdom Group
Took C.T. and N.S. in the late 1980s, and T.T.2 in 1992. Soul function is to help make Seventh Ray organization available to humanity.
Ginger hair in a casual "businessman's" cut.

Jarek Bogart – Crown Center of Wisdom Group
Studying NTFPW since the early 1980s, and teaching since mid '80s. Soul part of the First Ray "Leadership" center of the Wisdom Group.
Vaguely mediteranean/latin looking, about 5 foot 10 inches, heavyset.

Kelley Asa – Esoteric Healer
Serious Bailey student; MTCM (Master of Traditional Chinese Medicine) degree. Soul part of portion of Synthesis Ashram responsible for synthesizing East and West, in particular, approaches to healing.

Shoulder-length auburn hair, boyishly slender, pixyish face with tiny smile lines under eyes.

Mary Howell – Worker in Religion
M.A. in World Religions, associate pastor of a New Age Center. Soul's function is within the Throat Center of a Group Unit responsible for formulating the energy, force, and substance of a new *synthesizing* World Religion.

Maxwell (Max) – Synthesis Deva
Part of the new order of Synthesis Devas. Is charged with aiding and protecting Quinn. Primarily Indigo in color, with radiant indigo-white, violet-streaked "wings" fountaining back and up from his heart and brow.

Myron Oakley – Esoteric Anatomist
Studied Bailey, classic Theosophy, and did research at the Philosophical Research Society Library.

Short hair, florid complexion with rosacea on the back of his neck.

Nyle Tyndale – Esoteric Astrologer
Teaches Esoteric Astrology in the Los Angeles area and forming own online school—including yearlong course based on Bailey's "Labours of Hercules".

Wolfishly slender, graying "Luke Skywalker" hair with an Obiwan beard.

Quinn MacAndrews – Wisdom Group Heart Center
Took N.S. in 1973, and T.T. in 1974, and has studied, practiced, taught, and written about the Wisdom extensively. On Soul levels Quinn is a part of the nucleus of the Heart Center of the Wisdom Group (a Group Unit of

the Synthesis Ashram). He is currently focusing on precipitating the Wisdom into expressions that make it accessible to the mass of humanity.

Met his daughter Ellora for the first time only a week before the first workshop (Chapter 1), and prior to that had not known she existed.

Appearance: Quinn is fiftyish, slender, but not thin, a neat goatee, gold-washed wire rims, and light-brown combed-back hair.

Reva Levinthal – Healing Petal of Wisdom Group

C.T., N.S., and T.T. in the mid 1990s. Doctor of Chiropractic. Function to manifest the patterns of difficulty of the overall Group, resolve those patterns within herself, and help spread the solutions.

Mid to late thirties with a professional woman's short, brown hair, and a trim, shapely figure. Plain pantsuits that would look good under a white lab coat.

Zedekiah Selvyn (Zed) – Political Organizer

President of the Board of the Center where the workshops meet. Arcane School student in the 1970s. A dynamic and popular speaker.

Soul function is within the Heart Center of the "Leadership Group" of the Synthesis Ashram.

XII

Chapter 1

Prelude

A week after I found him, my dad took me to a workshop in the city. At first I thought it would be a boring bunch of bookwormy types getting all metaphory and revealy. But dad —we were so new then I still called him Quinn— said not, that it would be a 'practical demonstration of magic', and he wanted me to use my *sight* to see how it worked. It would help me learn how to use my abilities, how to do my work, and I could help him.[1]

It was a moonless night in a break and enterish neighborhood. We pulled out of a creepy alley into a parking lot behind an old office building —three stories with black iron bars over the lower windows. Vehicles were clustered around the entryway, blocking much of its light and casting long shadows over the lot.

Quinn slowly turned the 'cruiser's steering wheel, panning the headlights and checking for skulky types by the vehicles or in the raggedy bushes next to the building. The only life aura outside was the thin, sickly green clinging to the bushes, but I sent Chantel flying ahead to check.

Quinn parked in the empty center of the lot while Chantel scouted the perimeter and then flew into the building.

As we got out of the 'cruiser Quinn said, "Remember, these are good, intelligent people. We agree on a lot of things, but our approach is somewhat different. Some of them may feel threatened by that, and my inner work

---

[1] Quinn: At this time, Ellora was a fan of the "Buffy the Vampire Slayer" television series, and often used its slang in her private thoughts.

1

takes that into account. Watch what I'm doing, how they react, and what happens."

I was listening to him, and using my *sight* to watch Chantel through the cement-brick walls, so we were almost at the door before I spotted the keypad next to it. I froze, and Quinn wrapped his arm around my shoulders, above my pack, and gently said, "It's OK, the door opens automatically from the inside, just like a supermarket."

At that moment, the hallway flared with light as Chantel dropped through the ceiling, pulsing reassuring indigo-blue, and floated toward us—passing through the glass door like the light she is. I exhaled and relaxed my muscles, like Quinn was teaching me, and we started forward again.

It was just an ordinary office building where Quinn was giving a lecture, nothing like the Academy despite the lock. The glass door slid open with an easy sigh instead of the sullen squeal of an iron gate. Here, the distant sounds were office machines and polite voices, instead of frightened whispers and accusing stares. Chantel preceded us, glowing softly in my *sight*, up the stairs and down a long hall.

We stopped in front of an ordinary office door — nothing like the dark portal to the Headmaster's den— and it opened to reveal a cheerful room with over a dozen people seated about a large round table with crystals and a candle in the center, and posters and books around the walls. I took another breath, dismissed the image of Gran and Papo's tearful goodbye, and stepped inside.

The group quieted as we entered, and a tallish man in a leisure suit stood and beckoned us toward two empty chairs. His aura was dominated by reds, dark-brick at his tummy and clearing around his head. I knew he'd be a real stompy type but for the green

Chapter 1

streaks radiating from his heart.

I felt everyone looking at me as we walked around the table, but I was busy scanning the wall for electrical sockets. Finding one, I removed my pack, took out the recorder, and began setting it up.

I had to pause in the middle to be introduced. It was the first time, and I felt myself flush at "daughter" — they all knew Quinn was a bachelor. But their gazes were friendly, with a strong dose of pity —especially from the women. They'd obviously heard something about mom's accident, and my coming to live with Quinn. Chantel rushed in, quieted my heart and shrank the capithingies back to normal, and I managed a few polite noises.

None of them were *sighted*, so they didn't notice Chantel's entrance and departure, or the beings that arrived when Quinn sent an indigo-white stream of light upward from the center of his head —out of even my sight— and radiated light out from his head to the aura of the entire group.

I finished setting up and testing the recorder as he was forming an alignment back up, from the group aura to a higher source. Then I sat next to him, he stood, and I pressed the recorder's on button.

(Quinn relaxed as he spoke, his voice deepened and slowed, and most of the group responded by relaxing in turn.)

Quinn: "Well, first, I'd like to thank Zed and the rest of the board for inviting me to speak at the Center. As you know, a few years ago the Center began selling copies of books and booklets on something called 'The New Thought-form Presentation of the Wisdom', or 'the Wisdom', and allowing classes studying the materials to meet here. Since the Center has always focused primarily on the works of Alice A. Bailey, this was a somewhat controversial step. Since I've been teaching and practicing 'the Wisdom' for several decades, and have some knowledge of the Bailey works, I've been asked to facilitate workshops that explain this new 'Wisdom' material.

"What I propose to do is begin with the immediate — the practice of the Wisdom by the Spiritual Soul— and move to the Universal —the place and function of the Wisdom in the Divine Plan. We'll do this in a series of four workshops, beginning this evening with 'The Magic of Synthesis'.

"We will start by establishing an alignment with and invocation of the overshadowing Wisdom, and the success of our discussion will depend on our collective ability to maintain that alignment, despite any distractions that may arise. I will be speaking from that alignment, and I ask all of you to do so as well, formulating your questions and comments from within that alignment, and returning to it whenever you find yourself in another place or state of awareness.

(A number of people raised their hands. Several looked mildly bewildered or cast slightly cross looks. Some muddy yellow-orange entered the group aura, which was vibrating in an off-key chorus with a few points of clarity. Quinn warded their questions with slightly extended arms, palms out and down.)

"Now, I realize that you have many questions about what I mean by 'establishing and working from an alignment'. However, as that is the very subject of this evening's discussion, I suggest we begin by setting up the alignment, and then discuss what it is and how it works.

(Quinn folded himself into his chair, closed his eyes, and sat up straight with his arms in his lap, palms up. The group automatically followed suit, and after a few

Chapter 1

moments silence, Quinn began speaking quietly, calmly, with a rhythmic cadence.)

Opening Alignment

Relax the physical-dense body.
Calm the emotions.
Focus the mind.
Move up into the ajna center —approximately three inches in front of the forehead and between the brows— and there integrate the three-fold persona —body, emotions, and mind— into a single unit.

From —and remaining in— the ajna, align upward via a line of indigo-white through the crown center — approximately six inches above the head— to and with that portion of the Wisdom which overshadows this evening's discussion.

From the ajna, invoke that portion of the Wisdom downward into appearance by audibly sounding the OM. (long pause)

From the ajna, project that Wisdom outward to the group brain awareness by again audibly sounding the OM.

From the ajna, align the group brain upward, via a line of indigo-white light, directly to the overshadowing Wisdom —without going through your crown center. Again, audibly sound the OM. (pause)

Leaving this triangular alignment in place, slowly relax the attention and return to your normal focus, and open your eyes.

(Quinn waited until everyone appeared ready, and then began speaking.)

Chapter 1

The Magic of Synthesis

Quinn: "Our topic this evening is the Magic of Synthesis, beginning with the method, and concluding with the practical applications.

"Now 'magic', as I'm using the term, simply refers to the process by which all that exists is created. There are of course a number of ways of describing this process, and one of the easiest is to compare it to the Laws of Electromagnetism.

"The first expression of the One from which all comes may be compared to an electromagnet. Like the magnet, the One is also a Three, and it's via the interaction of all three that creation takes place.

(Quinn stood, walked over to the large dry-erase board mounted on one wall, and grabbed a purple marker. He drew as he spoke, and paused often to turn back to his audience and point with his marker. I took the digital camera out of my pack and got ready to capture the drawing.)

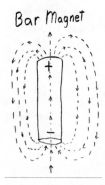

Bar Magnet

"Like the bar magnet, these Three Aspects of the One include a Positive Pole, a Negative Pole, and a magnetic field of relationship between the two poles. These three things —Positive Pole, Negative Pole, and Magnetic Field— are actually the first expression of that no thing from which all comes. These Three Aspects of Divinity function so much like an electromagnet that we may apply the scientific 'laws' of electromagnets to them:[2]

_____

[2] Glen: I suspect Quinn drew a bar magnet rather than an electromagnet because the bar magnet is easier to draw. The analogy works with either type of magnet.

"If you have one pole, you must have two poles.

"The two poles must always be equal in strength.

"If you have two poles, you must have a magnetic field.

"The strength of the magnetic field is determined by the strength of the poles and their distance from each other—the closer the poles, the more powerful the magnetic field."[3]

Kelley: "Why 'Positive' and 'Negative, why not 'North' and 'South'?"

Quinn: "Well, it would be confusing. Because of the way our compasses are traditionally marked, people in English speaking countries tend to associate 'North' with 'Positive' and 'South' with 'Negative'. However, that's incorrect. Earth's 'North' magnetic field is actually 'Negative' at present, while the 'South' is 'Positive.

"However, there are other terms. For instance, one can equate 'Positive to 'Yin' and 'Negative' to 'Yang' —in fact, I'll be including that perspective in one of my upcoming courses, *Raising the Queen of Heaven.* 'Positive' and 'Negative' simply happen to fit best with the electromagnet analogy."

Me: "At present?"

Quinn: "Hmm?"

Me: "Earth's magnetic field. You said 'at present'."

Quinn: "Oh. Yes. The Earth's magnetic field reverses every few thousand years. You can look it up tomorrow.[4]

"Now, since the entire creative process consists of the interaction between these Three, the Two Poles and the Magnetic Field, we may participate in that creative activity by manipulating the Three.

---

[3] Quinn: In the case of the Trinity, we might add, "the more powerful the magnetic field, the closer the poles."

[4] Ellora: About every 7,000 years.

Chapter 1

"The Seventh Ray approach is to manipulate the Three via Ceremonial Magic, or Divine Law and Order. We can do this because, being ourselves the magnetic field, and being therefore born *of* the Poles, we inherit the characteristics of the Three.

"Those characteristics include the focus of Intent of the Positive Pole, the Intelligent Activity of the Negative Pole, and the ability of the Magnetic Field to relate those Poles.

"Being born from a duality, that Magnetic Field is itself a duality, or two motions —an upward or 'ascent' motion and a downward or 'descent' motion.

"Via those motions, that magnetic field moves into and experiences union with each of its divine parents, an 'upper' union with the Positive Pole and a 'lower' union with the Negative Pole.

"Thus, the motion of the magnetic field or consciousness includes four stages, which D.K. describes as 'meditation with interludes'. This is the *Magic of Consciousness*, which is the primary meditation process taught in N.S. and utilized in the work of the Synthesis Ashram.[5]

"One can begin looking at that process from any point in it. However, since we are looking at the creative process from the perspective of the physical-dense brain, we normally begin at the low point, producing a basic outline of:

"Ascent

"Higher Interlude

"Descent

"Lower Interlude

---

[5] Quinn: N.S. = *The Nature of the Soul*, by Lucille Cedercrans

(Quinn gestured at his drawing as he spoke, stepped to the side to begin a new one, and I snapped a shot of the first.)

"Looking at it as a rotary motion, we can draw the complete cycle as something like this—

(Quinn drew a circle fairly low on the board, labeled it "persona", and continued speaking.) [6]

"Now, when explaining this process, in preparation for performing it, one generally uses symbolic terms such as:

"Ascent – internal magnetic field – Divine Daughter

"Higher Interlude – Positive Pole – Divine Father

"Descent – external magnetic field – Divine Son

"Lower Interlude – Negative Pole – Divine Mother

"Yes, Jed?"

Jed: "D.K. talks about that."

Arista: "That's right, in DINA and White Magic, as the breath of the consciousness." [7]

Quinn: "Yes, I've heard it's called both 'meditation with interludes', and 'the breath of the consciousness', but of course D.K. gives a more Second Ray perspective on it."

Arista: "What's the difference?"

Quinn: "In the perspectives? Well, it depends. In this case, Second emphasizes the point of greatest union —

---

[6] Quinn: "FM" = Full Moon and "NM" = New Moon.

[7] Glen: *Discipleship In The New Age, Vol. I*, p. 193, *Discipleship In The New Age, Vol. II*, pp. 452-53, p. 516, *A Treatise on White Magic*, p. 152, pp.515-18, and also in *From Intellect to Intuition*, pp. 141-42

the moment of absolute stillness at the interludes—
while Seventh emphasizes the Ceremonial Motion, particularly of the motivating principle.

"Yes, Nyle?"

Nyle: "Why do you call the, what, 'internal' field, the
'Daughter'?"

Quinn: "Actually, before humanity discovered electromagnetism or time, we used gender-specific personal
pronouns —the Divine Mother–Daughter–Father–Son
myth cycle, and they're still accurate. Look—

(Quinn stood stepped back up to
the dry-erase board, and drew two
new magnets, one showing the external field, and the other the internal
field.)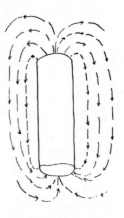

"Having at-oned with its over-
shadowing Divine Intent —a spark of
Spirit or of the Father Aspect— the
Soul descends.

"In the magnetic field analogy,
this descending consciousness is rep-
resented by the external, downward-
moving portion of the magnetic field.

"Now, having just at-oned with the Father, and
since it is at that point relating the Father to the
Mother, the characteristics of the Soul which are de-
rived from the Father are most apparent or predominant. The consciousness is then, in effect, masculine
during this descent and 'Divine Son' is the proper sym-
bolical term.

"So, the Divine Son/Soul conveys the Intent of Fa-
ther/Spirit to the Mother/Substance, and impresses that
Intent on Substance via at-one-ment.

"Then, having at-oned with Divine Intelligence or
Substance —the Mother Aspect— the Soul ascends. In

 the magnetic field analogy, this ascending Soul is represented by the internal, upward-moving portion of the magnetic field. Since it has just at-oned with Substance and is relating the Mother to the Father, the characteristics of the Soul which are derived from the Mother are predominant. The consciousness is then effectively feminine during this ascent and 'Divine Daughter' is an appropriate symbolical term.

"Arista?"

Arista: "Are you saying that creative magic occurs not only during the interludes between breaths, but during the breaths as well?"

Quinn: "Umm... Not quite. Remember, we're looking at this from a more Seventh Ray perspective, so the emphasis is on the entire process as a ceremony. From that perspective, the Ascent and Descent or upward and downward breaths are part of one ongoing process.

"If you focus on the interludes between breaths, then the breaths themselves may appear to be, well, interruptions or even annoyances — something to be eliminated. However, if you focus on the entire process as a ritual, then the Ascent or upward breath is what helps you achieve union with the Father, while the Descent or downward breath helps you achieve union with the Mother. The breaths are an active part of the ritual."

Arista: "Permanently?"

Quinn: "No. Once one reunites the two Poles, then the motion or breath between them stops. At that point, the consciousness has no need of the breath, because the breath was the cyclic interaction of Substance with the motivating Life. When those Aspects become One, Consciousness is liberated from that cycle.

(Several students raised their hands, and Quinn returned to his seat at the table.)

"Hold on, we'll discuss what that means in a bit.

"As long as it continues, the breath of the consciousness is just as much a part of the creative process as are
the interludes.

"Hal?"

Hal: "So then, the Soul creates via its breath with
interludes. But what about the other Aspects, aren't
they creative?"

Quinn: "Yes. Each Aspect is creative in its own way. So,
since there are Three Aspects, there are three basic types of
magic, each of which is characterized by its Aspect.

"For instance, what we usually think of when someone uses the term 'magic' is not The Magic of Consciousness, but the old Magic of Form —the sequential
activity of Divine Intelligence which produces new
forms. This type of magic was developed during the last
Seventh Ray age, in Atlantean times, and is the basis
for most of humanity's rituals up to now. The primary
difference between the two types is that while The
Magic of Consciousness uses the breath of consciousness, The Magic of Form uses the breath, or cyclic motion, of substance.

"In the old type of magic the consciousness moved or
progressed by identifying with a form, being carried
along by that form, and then identifying with another
form to be carried into the next experience."

Hal: "On purpose?"

Quinn: "Yes. This is how we incarnate. The Soul as-
sembles a persona, precipitates it into appearance,
moves into it, and is carried along by that form, gaining
a wealth of experience and wisdom in the process.

"This process of attachment continues throughout
the incarnation. The consciousness involved may be
participating in full awareness or, which is more often,

simply be carried along for the ride. However, the creative process doesn't stop.

It's like, well, do you all remember the Super Mario Brother's video game? My nephews used to play it in the 80's, and there were these little moving platforms that Mario and..."

Ellee: "Luigi."

Quinn: "Yes, Luigi had to jump onto and ride to a certain spot, before leaping onto another platform or back onto the trail.

"In The Magic of Form all forms of substance — mental, astral, physical-etheric, and physical-dense— work like those platforms. You identify with and become attached to them, and as they move they carry you along, until either that form stops moving —dies— or you jump off by attaching yourself to another form.

"Now, average humanity does this unconsciously, although that's changing, while the conscious 'magician' does it consciously. And that's what makes a magician a magician. They begin by learning how to detach from one form by attaching to another —like an inchworm moving from leaf to leaf— learn how to control the rhythms of forms a bit, and then, finally, learn how to create forms."

Kelley: "Aren't we supposed to detach from form?

Quinn: "Oh... That would be a long subject, and we don't really... Look, suppose the old Mir Space Station had a problem, and a cosmonaut has to go out to fix it. He suits up, goes through the lock, snaps a safety line onto an anchor ring, steps out, and his magnetic boots fail. He drifts to the end of his tether, and it snaps. So, there he is, drifting in space, completely detached from anything and everything, and totally, utterly helpless.

"Since the creative process involves the interaction of the Three, if you eliminate your relationship with any one of the Three then you can't *do* anything. So, basically, the whole 'detachment from form' thing is a huge glamour of the last age. It doesn't work, and it was never really the goal of spiritual paths of that age.

"Mary?"

Mary: "Then what was?"

Quinn: "Attachment."

Mary: "What? But—"

Quinn: "Remember how The Magic of Form works! You detach from one thing by attaching to another. So, in the Sixth Ray age of aspiration to a Spiritual Ideal..."

Mary: "They attached to Spirit!"

Quinn: "Yes, and worked to achieve unity or at-one-ment with it.[8]

Hal: "What about the whole 'form is evil' thing?"

Quinn: "A typical solar plexus reaction. Remember, the solar plexus divides everything into a polarity, and that which it identifies with it sees as 'good' and that which is different from that which it identifies with is seen as 'bad'. So, since humanity was polarized in its solar plexus, it experienced the Positive Pole —which they were aspiring to attach to— as 'good' and the Negative Pole —the opposite of their ideal— as 'bad'. None of that 'good' and 'bad' stuff was real, but it created lots of problems for the magician, and still does."

Nyle: "What kind of 'problems'?"

Quinn: "Well, for one thing, it's rather difficult to 'attach' to a new form if some part of you believes 'form is bad', and that the goal is 'detachment' from form. When you reach out for something, you wind up pushing it away, and when you finally grasp it, you find that your mental 'fingers' are slippery and won't grab hold."

---

[8] Quinn: See also the guru-chela relationship as discussed in Chapter 3.

Myron: "Are you saying evil does not exist?"

Quinn: "I'm saying that 'good' and 'bad' as conceived by the solar plexus are glamours. They're not real. There's a polarity behind them, but the solution to that polarity is in union not opposition."

Arista: "What about Black Magic, and the Forces of Light and Darkness?"

Quinn: "Um... Hold on a bit. We'll get to that.

"Now, ah..."

Me: "Detaching by attaching."

Quinn: "Right.

"Now, once a form is created —substance gathered and set into a particular motion— its life cycle is fixed. The cycles of its birth, growth, maturity, decline, and death are fixed from its beginning. Thus, once one identifies with and attaches to a form, unless you know how to alter its motion, it's going to take you wherever it's going. So, that's the basis of The Magic of Form, the ability to consciously:

"Choose what forms to attach to,

"Alter the motion of forms,

"Create forms that will take you where you want to go.

"Of course, the fact that the process involves attachment to substance means that the magician using that process has to work within the limits of substance.

Arista: "Can you give an example?"

Quinn: "Sure. Alcoholics Anonymous... Think about it. A Soul incarnates with patterns for and in an environment that predisposes them to substance abuse. Those patterns carry them toward destruction, until it become obvious to the consciousness trapped in those forms that they have to change. They attempt to detach from those patterns, but fail, and then succeed by attaching to the structure, and ritual motion, of a twelve-step program."

Arista: "*That's* magic?"

Quinn: "Oh, yes. A classic example —even includes surrendering to a 'higher power'."

Mary: "What about becoming so attached you can't detach?"

Quinn: "Well, you will detach eventually, in one incarnation or another. But, yes, it is possible to become over-attached to something —the magical traditions are full of cautionary tales. But, remember, there's a powerful sense of liberation that comes with the detachment of attachment, and it gets easier to do after the first time. However, the new magic goes beyond those limitations.

The Magic of Consciousness

Quinn: "Now, in the beginning at least, The Magic of Consciousness uses the same breath or cycle of relationship as The Magic of Form, but without attachment to form.

Nyle: "What? How—"

Quinn: "Hold on. I'll get to it.

"In other words:

"The *External* Magnetic Field relates the Intent of the Positive Pole to the Negative Pole, and,

"The *Internal* Magnetic Field relates the Intelligent Activity of the Negative Pole to the Positive Pole.

"However, instead of identifying with either Pole, the magnetic field identifies with the creative process — with the relationship between the Poles. This increased relationship brings the two Poles closer together, and — in keeping with the Laws of Electromagnetism— thereby strengthens the Poles and the Magnetic Field.

Arista: "Using the same cycle?"

Quinn: "As form? No, not necessarily. The Magic of Form has a rhythmic cycle or 'breath" because it involves the identification of consciousness with form. Since all substance moves in cycles or breaths, and consciousness takes on the characteristics and limits of any form it identifies with, The Magic of Form both works through and is limited to the breath of substance.

Arista: "But the new magic isn't?"

Quinn: "That's right. Since The Magic of Consciousness does not involve the identification of consciousness with substance, the consciousness of the magician does not become identified with and caught up in either the form or the breath of the form, but remains free to continue practicing the creative process.

Hal: "Wait... What was that about making the Poles stronger?"

Quinn: "Well, you all know the basic nature of each of the Three Aspects?

(Heads nodded all around the table.)

"The First Aspect or Positive Pole is the source of Divine Purpose, Power, and Will. This is the Life, the source of the motivating impulse for *all that is*.

"The Third Aspect or Negative Pole is the source of Intelligent Activity. That Intelligent Activity differentiates the One into the many, producing —if the consciousness identifies with one of those differentiated parts— awareness of separation, the experience of being separate and apart.

"The Second Aspect or Magnetic Field *is* the relationship between the First and Third Aspects, and thus it is its nature to relate things, to bring the differentiated parts back into a condition of union or at-one-ment.

Chapter 1

"So, if you practice The Magic of Form you are creating?"

(Quinn paused and slowly glanced around the table. Parts of the group aura sort of reached upward along the line of light Quinn had created, while other parts did not respond, and some sort of pushed the new light away.)

Myron: "Separation?"

Quinn: "No, *differentiation*. There's a very fine distinction there, but it's important. Look, take, say, 'liberals' and 'conservatives' in the political arena.

"We may define liberals as those who are responsible for breaking down barriers and enabling government to grow into new arenas. Without that growth government would stagnate and die, but if that growth went unchecked government would quickly grow beyond its ability to support itself, and collapse.

"On the other hand, conservatives may be defined as those who are responsible for maintaining the established structures and limits of government. Without that maintenance the government would collapse, but if the structure becomes so rigid it prevents growth and movement the government will stagnate and die.

"Thus, both growth and maintenance are needed.

"Now, the same is true in The Magic of Form. New forms must be created while old forms are maintained. So long as both functions work together, in service to the larger life of which they are a part, then all is well. If they struggle against each other, or one overwhelms the other, then there will be problems.

Amanda: "So neither is good or bad, but either may be... out of right relationship with the larger life?"

Quinn: "Yes."

Arista: "But Black Magic is different, isn't it?"

Quinn: "Oh my, yes. That's... Well, let's build the foundation a bit more before we get to that.

"Now, umm...

Me: "'If you're doing The Magic of Form...'"

Quinn: "Right. So, if you're performing the old Magic of Form, the interaction of the Two Poles via that magic continues the differentiation process —the growth and development of Substance and of the Consciousness in that Substance.

"Now, so long as one is working to create forms to carry the consciousness to the next step in its evolution, and/or to embody the Intent of the One Life, then everything is fine. The focus is on the growth and development of Consciousness, and that's White Magic.

"However, when one is working to perfect form for its own sake, irrespective of the Intent of the One Life but for one's own purposes, then that's Black Magic."

Arista: "So it's the intent?"

Quinn: "Yes. The type of magic —Form or Consciousness— is irrelevant to whether it's 'White' or 'Black'. The essential point is the intent behind the creative process.

"Now, to continue with The Magic of Consciousness; in the beginning, at least, this type of magical activity has it own rhythm, the motion of the consciousness between the poles. As we've discussed, D.K. refers to this several times as 'meditation with interludes' — although not, as I recall, in those exact words— thereby placing the emphasis on the points of stillness.

"However, due to a more Seventh Ray perspective, *Nature of the Soul* and the related materials focus on the overall process, in terms of the ascent, upper interlude, descent, and lower interlude.

Arista: "But it's the same thing?"

Quinn: "It's the same meditation process, but the intent and thus the effects are quite different."

Zed: "Different how? Could you go into that a bit more?"

Chapter 1

Quinn: "Oh, well... many of you are in a far better position than I to characterize the Bailey —meditation with interludes— approach, so I'll focus on what I know from my own experience.

"While the creative work of the consciousness is done during the interludes —the high and low points of absolute stillness— the ascent and descent are an absolutely crucial and often overlooked part of the process. Look at what happens at each point:

"During the Lower Interlude, the Overshadowing Intent is conveyed to and impressed on Substance. Substance responds with a 'new' Intelligent Activity —actually a modification of or adjustment to its earlier activity.

"During the cyclic motion of Ascent, the focus of attention of the devas of the lower three —the physical-etheric, astral-emotional, and mental— are turned upward toward the Soular Deva, and the consciousness in the lower three is prepared for at-one-ment with the Overshadowing Spiritual Soul.

"During the Upper Interlude, the devas of the lower three touch or unite with —depending on the level of development— the Soular Deva, and the incarnate consciousness touches or at-ones-with the Overshadowing Soul. At that moment of absolute stillness, the consciousness grasps the Will or Intent of the Soul.

"During the Descent, the consciousness and its associated devic substance project that Intent downward into expression in each of the three lower worlds — with the consciousness tuning to the frequency of each realm and sounding the note of that Intent into it, and the devic substance embodies that Intent in each realm via a cyclic rhythm.

Myron: "What's this 'soular deva'?"

Quinn: "The Light Body of the Soul, that portion of buddhic substance which is attracted to the Soul when it first sounds the creative word, is set in motion when it sounds the word a second time, and shattered when it sounds it a third time.

Arista: "That's not the egoic lotus."

Quinn: "No. There's a relationship, but we really don't have time to go into that this evening."

Myron: "So devas are part of the process?"

Quinn: "Of course. It's a mutual effort, with the two kingdoms working together hand-in-hand so to speak.

"However, you will note that in this process the consciousness is, in a sense, directing the attention and ordering the activity of the devas. Thus, the consciousness is the actor rather than that which is acted upon.

"One may compare this to the difference between surfing a wave and creating the wave that others surf. The surfer has to go to the right place, and wait for a wave of the right shape and size that happens to be going in the proper direction. However, in The Magic of Consciousness the Soul directs the devas to create the necessary waves, without necessarily becoming a 'surfer' itself.

Myron: "You've talked about waves, rhythms, and breaths, but what are they?"

Quinn: "Oh... Well, the rhythms of the magical process include such things as daily, lunar, and annual meditation cycles, each with their own ascent and descent phases.

Annual Cycles

"For instance, in the annual cycle the ascent phase is in the first half of the year and the descent or manifestation phase is the second half. Thus, in an annual rhythm one would emphasize the ascent portion of the work during the first sixth months, and the descent portion during the second half. That's why, for instance, Wisdom Impressions usually publishes Lucille's works in the Fall. In the preceding Spring the emphasis was on the preparatory subjective work.

Lunar Cycles

"Within each year, each lunar cycle also has its breaths or rhythms.

"The inbreath or Ascent is the two-week period from New Moon to Full Moon. During this period the focus of the creative work is on ascending, via aspiration, toward union with the overshadowing idea or purpose.

"The Full Moon is the 'first' interlude, the pause between inhaling or ascent and exhaling or descent. During this period the focus of the creative work is on at-oneing with the idea or purpose, identifying with it without interpreting it.

"The outbreath or Descent is the two-week period from Full Moon to New Moon. During this period the focus of the creative work is on precipitating the idea or purpose into the mental, astral, and physical-etheric, where the devas of those planes formulate it into organized patterns of energy, force, and substance.

"The New Moon is the 'second' interlude, the pause between exhaling or descent and inhaling or ascent. During this period the focus of the creative work is on recognizing or observing the completed work —without identifying with it.

Daily Cycles

"Now, within each moon each day has its breaths, and it's here that we have our most immediate or 'everyday' experience of those rhythms. There are of course a number of ways to break it down, but one way is as follows:

"The inbreath or Ascent is the twelve hour period from midnight to noon. During this period the focus of the creative work is on ascending, via aspiration, toward union with the purpose or idea of the day.

"Noon is the 'first' interlude, the pause between inhaling or ascent and exhaling or descent. The focus of meditations performed at this time is on identifying with that purpose without interpreting it.

"The outbreath or Descent is the twelve hour period from noon to midnight. During this period the focus of the creative work is on precipitating the day's purpose.

"Midnight is the 'second' interlude, the pause between exhaling or descent and inhaling or ascent. The focus of meditations performed at this time is on observing the completed work without identifying with it.[9]

"Of course these cycles of the day include lesser cycles, but the sum of all of these cycles within cycles is 'the Ceremony of Life', and every true practitioner of the Magic of Consciousness practices that Ceremony in their own way.[10]

(A muddy yellow fog crept into the lower group aura, which began sounding an insistent, off-key tone – like an old-fashioned phone.)

Hugh: "That's totally impractical. You'd have to completely restructure your entire life! Who'd do that!"

Myron: "No kidding, DINA advises regular daily meditation but not to the point of regimenting every hour of every day!"

---

[9] Glen: Typically done while sleeping. See – *The Nature of The Soul*, pp. 293 - 294

[10] Glen: See also – *Leadership Training*, by Lucille Cedercrans, pp. 34 – 37

Chapter 1

(Quinn began radiating clear golden-yellow light outward from the center of his head, through his brow, to the auras of the group.)

Quinn: "Actually, that sort of restructuring of one's life and affairs around the work is a normal and necessary part of the path, part of the discipline of discipleship.

"Besides, you're really intensely aware of the cycles, especially the daily one's, only in the beginning. They gradually blend together as you practice them, until one's entire life and affairs becomes a moving picture of the life of the Soul."

Celine: "The 'Ceremony of Life'."

Quinn: "That's what N.S. calls it, yes."

Mary: "I really don't see... What's the point, what makes these cycles work?"

Quinn: "Well, let's look at lunar cycles. One way to approach the way they work is to compare them to merry-go-rounds. Have all of you ridden one, one of the big old ones with music and painted wooden horses that go up and down?

(All the older people raised their hands, and most of the younger one's. But as Quinn glanced over everyone he saw that I had not. His heart pulsed a pale, sad blue for a moment, steadied, and he moved on.)

"They used to have a nice one at Pacific Ocean Park —before they tore the place down— and there was another good one at Knott's Berry Farm.

"Some of the old merry-go-rounds had a post standing next to them, with a large brass ring hanging from the post, and kids —well, boys mostly— would lean out and try to 'grab the brass ring' as they went by.

"This may have started as a survival of the old knightly training method of tilting, in which knights would train themselves to hold the tip of their lance steady enough, at a full gallop, to pass the tip of the lance through such a ring. Thus, grabbing a ring while riding a 'horse' was an ancient sign of manly skill, which survived into the twentieth century as 'grabbing the brass ring' while 'mounted' on a merry-go-round.

(Quinn turned his chair and, pretending the round table we were seated around was a merry-go-round, and his chair was a horse, acted out his description as he spoke —moving up and down in his chair, and gripping the table with one hand while he reached out and grabbed with the other.)

"Anyway, the reason it's so difficult to grab the brass ring is that it appears to be coming at you with a relative velocity of say, fifteen, twenty miles an hour, while you're also moving up and down. You have to estimate where the ring is going to be, place your hand there, and then grab the ring off its hook —without losing your precarious grip on your leaping mount.

"So, you're spinning around, your mount is bouncing up and down, and with one hand gripping the pole and the corresponding leg hooked over the saddle you lean out, reach with your free hand, grab the ring, flip it up over the hook and you have it!

(Quinn held an imaginary ring up in triumph, paused, then turned his chair back toward the table and resumed speaking.)

"Now, grasping an overshadowing Divine Concept is rather like that —all the twisty, bucky, hard to grasp parts. However, there's a secret, well, a trick really, that makes the whole process much easier.

"You see, the idea or 'brass ring' is actually being held out to us by someone who wants us to have it. They're sitting on another merry-go-round, which is rotating in the opposite direction, counterclockwise to your clockwise, and there's a way we can use our relative motion to make the handoff easy.

Chapter 1

(Quinn stood, stepped up to the board, drew a second circle above the earlier one, and turned to face the group.)

"Depending on how you look at it, this illustration is either a drawing of the cycles of the Soul and of the Persona, or a drawing of two merry-go-rounds, turning in opposite directions and seen from above.

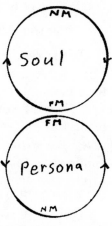

"Now, let's say that it's merry-go-rounds for a moment, and that from our perspective the one on top is turning clockwise while the one on bottom is turning counterclockwise. Each of the merry-go-rounds has a rider, and the rider on the top one is trying to hand off a brass ring, the 'Ring of Truth' (groans), to the rider on the bottom merry-go-round. Both merry-go-rounds are turning at the same rate of speed, in opposite directions, and the riders' horses are going up and down at the same time.

"So, given all that, at the point of nearest approach —at the Full Moon— the riders will, for a moment, be moving parallel to each other at the same speed and will, for that moment, *appear stationery* to each other while within arms reach. All the upper rider with the ring would have to do is reach out and hand it over.

(Quinn returned to his chair, sat, and gazed around the table.)

"The Magic of Consciousness works very much like that.

"The Soul is in meditation deep throughout the incarnation process, and, in a quite literal sense, the Ascent–Meditation–Descent cycles of the persona are a reflection or 'mirror image' of the Ascent–Meditation–Descent cycles of the Soul. Thus:

27

During the New Moon the Soul is at its Higher Interlude and the persona is at its Lower, and

At the Full Moon the Soul is at its Lower Interlude while the Persona is at its upper.

If the two reach the point of closest approach at the same time, they will be going in the same direction, and, for a moment, each will appear motionless to the other.

"Thus, if you coordinate your meditation cycles, to bring the incarnate consciousness to its highest point of receptive stillness at the precise moment when the overshadowing and incarnate Soul is closest, then the higher can be transferred to the lower with ease!"

Arista: "But... It can't be that easy!"

Quinn: "How difficult is it to re-order your life?

"Like most such things it's incredibly simple in conception, but very difficult in application. Part of what makes it difficult *now* is that this is a Seventh Ray creative activity of the consciousness. We're accustomed to a more Sixth Ray creative activity of Substance, and the differences can be quite confusing."

Hugh: "Like what?"

Quinn: "Oh, we'll cover part of that next week, when we discuss Organization. In the meantime, contemplate how the old Sixth Ray paths emphasized the Ascent portion of the creative cycle, and often neglected or even rejected the Descent. Many times the Seeker would withdraw from contact with the outer world, and attempt to ascend to unity with the Divine. The problem was that because of the way the cycles work, *you can't have an Ascent without a Descent.*"

(Quinn paused again and gazed around the table, radiating indigo-white light like a lighthouse into a still and silent night.)

Celine: "What goes up must come down."

Chapter 1

Quinn: "Yes. In this case kicking and struggling all the way, because they saw the Descent as a kind of falling out of union with the Divine."

Mary: "Falling from grace."

Quinn: "In Christian terms, yes.

"Now, however, the predominating Seventh Ray of this age places an increasing emphasis on the Descent part of the cycle, while maintaining the recognition of the Ascent, so that the new spiritual practices can include a balance of both.

Hugh: "What did that old emphasis do?"

Quinn: "Well, one of the difficulties we have is that our intellectual ideals, modern educational system, etc., have taught us to gather all the pertinent information, analyze it, and make a decision on the basis of an intelligent plan. However, from the perspective of the Overshadowing Soul that's not what the rational mind is for. The throat center is *not* a decision-making organ, but a mechanism of intelligent organization.

"During the ascent process the rational mind helps organize the lower instrument and hold its focus on the overshadowing ideal or idea of Truth.

"During the descent process the rational mind helps organize the precipitating idea into a plan of action.

"It does not 'decide' so much as help carry out the decision."

Nyle: "So how do you know..."

Quinn: "You *discover* what to do by working the creative process.

"Look, you can all see that I don't have any notes in front of me, and all I knew before I arrived was the general subject of the workshop. However, over the last couple lunar cycles I've been relating this group with the overshadowing portion of the Wisdom, and the over-shadowing Wisdom with this group, working to increase the relationship. And now, here, via that relationship I'm formulating the descending Wisdom into words."

Amanda: "So, you're explaining the Magic of Consciousness by doing it?"

Quinn: "Yes, certainly. Otherwise it would be, well, depending on where one was in one's instrument, either an intellectual treatise or a mystical sermon, neither of which could embody or convey the Idea."

Angelique: "What about meditations?"

Quinn: "You mean formulating them? That works the same way. Depending on the situation, you may do some preparatory work ahead of time, or you may do everything on the spot, but you're working the same basic process. If it's a group med, or one you'll be doing again over a lunar cycle say, then you'll formulate it into words as you work each step of the Ascent–Meditation–Descent–Embodiment process for the first time. Then you write it down and everybody performs it for that cycle."

Hal: "'Meditation' and 'embodiment'?"

Quinn: "Oh, those are the terms used in Lucille's stuff for what happens during the upper and lower interludes."

Arista: "How do you know when to do this, to work the magical process?"

Quinn: "Well, eventually you do it constantly, twenty-four hours a day, seven days a week. Of course, that doesn't usually happen all at once, but develops slowly. Normally one begins with scheduled meditations, at set times and places, say at home in the morning and evening —with emergency adjustments done where and as needed— then one slowly expands the number of scheduled meds and the situations in which one performs unscheduled exercises —while washing

Chapter 1

the dishes, working out, etc. Eventually you wind up practicing a formless meditation constantly, bringing the two Poles into closer alignment with every thought, word, and action."

Ellee: "*All* the time? Even while driving?"

Quinn: "I performed three meditations on the freeway on the way here. One was an adjustment of current events, and another was part of my preparation for this workshop. Of course, I'm quite familiar with the route and I've been meditating long enough that I could place the persona on 'autopilot' until it's time to exit or something comes up."

Ellee: "Is that safe?"

Quinn: "My daughter was with me." (Indicating that he wouldn't if it wasn't.)

"It's simply a matter of working the inner process long enough that you can do it and something else without thinking about it, like walking and talking at the same time. Your consciousness is doing one thing while your persona is doing something else. If something comes up, your persona will call you back.

"And that's a very important point. In The Magic of Consciousness, while the self does not become attached to the forms it inhabits, or to those it creates, it's still responsible for them, and thus observes and responds to what it observes as necessary."

Nyle: "What happens next, after the 24/7 meditation?"

Quinn: "Well, it's a gradual process. Eventually, when the Overshadowing Spiritual Soul and the incarnate soul merge and become one, the upper and lower interludes become one as well. At that point, the 'breath of the Soul' ceases. One dwells apart from the cycles or breaths, observing but not participating in them as they wash around and through you without disturbing you."

Myron: "When is that, what initiation?"

Quinn: "Oh, let's hold off on that until the third workshop, on Group Discipleship.

"So, then the Three in you become one, and you move on from the magic of the Second Aspect to what we could call the magic of the First Aspect.

The Magic of Spirit

Quinn: "The third of these three types of creative activity is The Magic of Spirit, or that of the First Aspect. Now, there's not really very much I can say about this, as I have very little experience with it and am still formulating that into words.

"At the point where one begins to practice this, one has left behind both the sequential intelligent activity of substance and the at-oneing relationship of Soul, and, having united one's Substance and Consciousness with Divine Intent, have become a single magnetic point from and to which all flows. It is as though the poles of a magnet had been combined, producing an extremely powerful —radiant and attractive— monopole."

Hugh: "A monad?"

Quinn: "Umm... Let's stick with mono-pole."

Nyle: "Does it include the same types of rhythms?

Quinn: Well, in a way, yes, it's another mirror.

(Quinn stood, walked up to the board and drew a third circle above the earlier two, and then faced the group.)

"However, this is deceptive, because in itself the Spirit does not utilize these rhythms any more than the re-united Soul

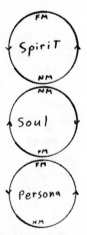

Chapter 1

does. So, what this really is is how the cycles work from the perspective of the Soul that still uses cycles.

(Zed tapped his watch, indicating that it was time to wrap things up.)

"So, what we have then are three types of magic:

The Magic of Form,

The Magic of Consciousness, and

The Magic of Spirit.

The Magic of Consciousness uses the breath of the Soul to reunite the Poles of Divinity, and is the primary type of magic in this Seventh Ray age.

"Next week, we'll explore 'Organization in the New Age'.

"Any final questions?

"OK, let's close with a meditation."

Closing Meditation

Quinn: "As a group, renew the upward line of indigo-white light from the group ajna, through the group crown center, to the Wisdom and that portion of the Wisdom overshadowing the group. (pause)

"As a group in the ajna, invoke that portion of the Wisdom downward, through the three lower worlds and into the group brain awareness, by audibly sounding the OM. (long pause)

"From the ajna, project that Wisdom outward into appearance in the group life and affairs by again audibly sounding the OM. (long pause)

"From the ajna, align the group brain upward, via a line of indigo-white light, back up to the overshadowing Wisdom. Again, audibly sound the OM. (pause)

"Leaving the alignment in place, slowly relax the attention and return to this here and now.

Chapter 1

Postscript

His aura had shrunken inward an inch or so, paled slightly, and the rotation was slower, almost sluggish. I wondered if his work always depleted him this much, or if it was just this class. We'd been back on the freeway a while, and were passing an "LAX" exit sign, when he finally said, "How was it?"

"Not so bad. Scary at first, but they're nice people, like you said, and Amanda, Mrs. Flintwright, was there."

"She wanted you to see a familiar face."

"It helped. Will we visit her again soon?"

"Next month."

He went quiet for a bit, until we'd switched to another freeway. Then he asked, "What did you see?"

"They all have some, well, higher? relationship to what you're talking about, don't they?"

"Yes. Each in their own way."

"I can't *see* that, but there's something —different shapes or thingys— in each of them that react to what you say."

"React how?"

"Well, differently. Some thingys sort of resonate and get brighter, others darken and slow, and some get really noisy and icky.

"Pay close attention to those, the 'icky' ones. Some will get bigger and stronger, and become a nuisance before they're dissipated."

"How will you do that?"

"Watch. Listen also, but we'll have the tapes, so mostly watch."

He stayed quiet then, and I watched the lights of people in passing cars the rest of the way home.

The Magic of Consciousness – Workshops

Chapter 2

Organization in the New Age

Zed flashed a fakey smile and beckoned us forward, into the group aura. I felt queasy and wanted to run, but I saw Amanda forcing her frail body to stand, so I rushed forward to help her up. She enfolded me in a motherly embrace, and the other women smiled their acceptance. She released me after a bit, and I helped her sit and began setting up my equipment. Quinn began working the table like a city councilman at a PTA meeting. I was too far away to hear clearly, but Chantel floated over and relayed it to me.

Quinn consoled Hal for a breakup with his girl-friend, and I saw that Hal's aura was more disturbed than it had been.

Quinn exchanged a few words with Zed about group finance and promised to call later, cooed over pictures of Mary's new grandchild, and congratulated Reva on the success of a fundraiser.

When I was all set, he worked his way to his chair and sat, and formulated the same alignment he'd used last week. I turned on the recorder.

Opening Alignment

Relax the physical-dense body.
Calm the emotions.
Focus the mind.
Move up into the ajna center, and there integrate the three-fold persona into a single unit.

From (and remaining in) the ajna, align upward via a line of indigo-white through the crown center to and with that portion of the Wisdom which overshadows this evenings workshop.

From the ajna, invoke that portion of the Wisdom downward into appearance by audibly sounding the OM. (long pause)

From the ajna, project that Wisdom outward to the group brain awareness by again audibly sounding the OM.

From the ajna, align the group brain upward, via a line of indigo-white light, directly to the overshadowing Wisdom (without going through your crown center). Again, audibly sound the OM. (pause)

Leaving this triangular alignment in place, slowly relax the attention and return to your normal focus.

Chapter 2

Organization in the New Age

Quinn: "Well, I see several faces that weren't here last week. Larry, I understand Grace is recovering? Good! I hope the essences helped.

"Did everyone who wasn't here last week get to hear the tape? Yes? OK.

"Well, as you'll recall, our first workshop focused on 'The Magic of Synthesis', in particular the Seventh Ray creative process as it's being worked today. Now, in this evening's workshop we'll be looking at the way the creative process —both the old Magic of Form and the new Magic of consciousness— works in organizations.

"However, before we get into that, we'll need to look into what we mean by an 'organization'.

"Does anyone have any ideas?"

Zed: "A group who work together for a common goal."

Quinn: "Very good. Let's go with that.

(Quinn stood while speaking, and stepped up to the drawing board.)

"The key words there are 'group', 'work', and 'goal', so let's contemplate those.

(Quinn added pulses of indigo-indigo, green, and red to the group alignment as he spoke.)

"First, I'd suggest that a group is any collection of distinct parts that together make a larger whole. Now, you'll note that from this perspective, the human persona is a group consisting —when integrated into a whole— of the Mental, astral, and physical-etheric instruments, reflected into the physical-dense.

Myron: "The persona isn't a group until it integrates?"

Quinn: "Not under this definition. Until then it's a collection of related bodies and organs working somewhat at cross-purposes. It doesn't become a functioning group until the various parts begin to work cooperatively. Now, we'll explore the various parts of a functioning group next week, but in the meantime we may consider that the integration process includes:

Formulating the different goals of the parts into a single, unified purpose.

Directing all the parts to act together in carrying out or manifesting that purpose.

Under this definition an organization consists of a group, united by a single purpose and expressing that purpose via united activity. Thus, an organization is united by purpose, identity, and activity. (Another pulse of red with 'purpose', indigo-indigo with 'identity', and green with 'activity'.)

Celine: (Absorbing and 'recognizing' the colors.) "All Three Aspects."

Quinn: "Yes. An organization is a unity of all Three Aspects. However, the emphasis or balance between those Three changes with humanity's growth and development and with the ages.

Celine: "As with the current conflict, between Sixth and Seventh."

Quinn: "Yes. That apparent conflict is quite interesting, and very pertinent to our concept of organizations. All of the teachings of the last age were qualified with Sixth Ray to some degree, whether they were 'faith based' —aspiration to truth via belief— or 'knowledge' based —aspiration to truth via knowledge.

"The incoming Seventh Ray, however, is moving humanity toward the ceremonial magic of consciousness, or what we might call 'magic based' practices. One result is that both 'faith' and abstract 'knowledge' — knowledge for the sake of knowledge— seem increasingly unsatisfactory.

Mary: "But is faith really waning? Look at the rise of

religious conservatism."

Quinn: "Actually, in a way, the rise in fundamentalism is a sign of this waning. Remember I discussed liberalism and conservatism last week as those who create the new and those who preserve the old. Well, both of those poles tend to run to their extremes when they feel they're under attack. So, that extremism is a defensive reaction, in this case it's an attempt to protect traditional religious beliefs.

Hugh: "So they're defending themselves?"

Quinn: "It feels that way to them. They've identified with something —a religion, values, way of life— and because those are changing, while others are arriving, they feel like theirs are threatened or under attack. So they defend themselves by attacking back. It's part of the whole identification-with-form thing.[11]

"Of course, religion isn't really under attack so much as it's changing in response to the incoming Seventh Ray impulse. But the crystallized form can't tell the difference between transformation and destruction, and since the religious are identified with and as that form, they can't either.

"Keep in mind that Sixth and Seventh aren't really in conflict. The appearance of conflict arises when the old forms come into contact with the new, the old refuses to adjust, and the new has to make a place for

---

[11] Quinn: According to national, scientific surveys, although the total adult population of the United States went up by 32.5 million between 1990 and 2000, only 8 million were new Christians. Thus, the percentage of the adult population who identified themselves as "Christian" dropped from 86.2% in 1990 to 76.5% in 2000. During that period "New Age" went up 340%, but that figure is deceptive. It represents a move from only 1.14% of the adult population to 3.27%, and does not include "Spiritualists", "Druids", "Wiccans" or others.

itself —within our personal, group, and planetary lives.

Resolving this apparent conflict is part of the work immediately ahead of us, particularly for those with Sixth and/or Seventh rays predominant somewhere in their instrument —individual or group— as they will tend to experience it most acutely."

Nyle: "Unfortunately, not only were the teachings of the Piscean Age built under the Sixth Ray cycle, but since Earth's humanity incarnated through that cycle for the last 2000 years, we're still very influenced by it and habitually become devoted and attached to our chosen 'New Age' teachings."

Quinn: "Ummm... I'd be careful about calling the Sixth Ray influence 'unfortunate'. Yes, Sixth Ray permeated everything in the last age, but while humanity often interpreted that in a very polarized way, it still had many benevolent effects. And those effects, the ability to ideate, to focus on abstractions, to transcend the three lower worlds, all of that will remain with us if we do not reject the whole thing.

"Remember the way polarity works! One can't reject one pole without automatically rejecting the other, and that's not our function in the One Life anyway. It's the devas job to differentiate, it's our job to relate, to bring poles into unity. And we do that, as groups, via the Magic of Consciousness.

"Yes, while Sixth Ray is waning it's still quite powerful and its forms persist and continue to have their effects. But the tendency to take the Sixth Ray approach is also waning, more so with each generation born under the Seventh Ray impulse, which makes it necessary to renew and expand the expressions of the *New Thoughtform Presentation*.

"Today's humanity is both more receptive to the Wisdom than previously, and stands in need of presentations that are more permeated with Seventh Ray than was heretofore possible.

"This is a bit technical, but the entire Sixth Ray approach —as it has come to us— should be considered in the context of the Third Ray civilization of which it was a part. The disciples of the past age were —quite properly— endeavoring to build the *forms* —mental, astral and physical-dense— that would bring the Divine Plan to humanity.

"However, the disciples of this age are endeavoring to precipitate the plan in a Seventh Ray age, via a new Seventh Ray civilization. If we manage this by transforming the old civilization, not destroying it, then the focus will remain on the inner magical creative activity of consciousness. When we do this, the entire life and affairs becomes a moving picture of the inner state of consciousness —to paraphrase N.S. When the consciousness is *of love*, then the outer life is a moving picture of love.

"Hugh?"

Hugh: "What attracted me to Lucille's work from the beginning is its hands-on, practical approach to applying the Wisdom in our everyday lives. I tried to study the Ageless Wisdom for years, but it was just a head-trip, and I didn't feel like I got anywhere. Then I found *The Nature of the Soul* and there was this instant connection."

Quinn: "A lot of people have had that kind of experience with Lucille's material, especially regarding its 'hands-on practical approach'. Now, there are a couple things to keep in mind when we have that sort of experience with a presentation. Our reaction to that presentation is an expression of both the Ray behind that work, and of our primary Ray of approach *to* that work. For instance, a Fifth Ray approach to a Sixth Ray religion will usually produce a rejection of the religion. That does not mean that either is right or wrong, merely not particularly compatible at that point.

"Sixth Ray is presently waning in influence while Seventh is waxing. Any form of expression of the Ageless Wisdom which was formulated during the past age will be permeated with Sixth Ray, and the methods of approach to Truth, the Path itself as formulated during that age, was also permeated with Sixth Ray. Thus, in the Sixth Ray age of the philosopher, we had teachings which were 'about' truth, and methods of walking the Path which directed one's attention inward away from the world of affairs and upward toward abstract ideals and ideas.

"During the Sixth Ray age, the emphasis was on using Sixth Ray methods to gain abstract realization. In the case of Christianity it was abstract realization and/or endlessly detailed theological arguments over the philosophy of the Second Ray teachings of The Christ. Access to First or Seventh Ray teachings was a bit more difficult during that age, and even the followers of those Seventh Ray paths tended to approach them as abstract ideas.

"Now there is nothing wrong with any of this. It was simply an expression of where humanity, and the entire planetary life, was at that time.

"However, as we move into this Seventh Ray age, the emphasis is naturally shifting from aspiration to abstract ideas to that magical activity of consciousness which manifests Divine Intent. Lucille's works are an expression of the Synthetic Ashram. That Ashram was formulated by synthesizing First, Second, and Seventh. In particular, her work is an expression of the Seventh Ray aspect of the Synthetic Ashram, and carries the synthesizing quality of that Ashram. Thus, the emphasis in those works is on performing the ceremonial

44

magic of consciousness, on the work of group discipleship rather than on abstract knowledge."

Zed: "You'll explain about the Ashram later?"

Quinn: "In the fourth workshop, yes."

"Now, naturally the new Synthesis energy, the new
path of group initiation, and the new Synthesis Ashram
are easier for some to understand than for others. For
instance, those who are part of the new Ashram on Soul
levels are particularly receptive. However, that does not
mean that they are in any way more 'advanced' on the
path.

"It is a peculiarity of this stage of transition from
Sixth to Seventh, from the old path to the new, that
those who have advanced furthest down the old path of
individual realization, who in a sense have the most
invested in it, have the most difficulty recognizing the
new path of group initiation.

"Imagine, for instance, a disciple along First Ray
lines who, along the old path, has passed through the
halls of Experience, of Knowledge, and of Initiation, has
taken the first, and second initiations and is standing
before the door at the culmination of the third, preparing to become a world leader and server. Under the new
path of group initiation, the First Ray path is via cooperative leadership, of which he has no knowledge or
experience. In order to take initiation via the new path,
this candidate for initiation would have to retrace his
steps down the mount of initiation, releasing everything
he had learned, giving up his embodied capacity to
serve, and begin again as a novice. Most simply do not
see a need to do so.

"Now this is not a fault, it's more Newton's third law
of motion as applied to the Soul on the Path —an object
in motion will tend to continue in that same motion
until acted upon by an external force. Difficult as it is, it

is much easier for a Soul which is just beginning the path to participate in group initiation than it is for that Soul which has already journeyed some distance down —or up— the path of individual realization.

Myron: (With a judgy olive-blue around his throat, vibrating to a discordant G-Flat.) "Initiates would be more flexible."

Quinn: "It's not a question of flexibility, but capacity. A disciple or initiate who came up through the old path would have no embodied capacity to serve via the new. Also, in some ways it's better for those on the new path that the disciples and initiates of the old move on. Remember, those 'advanced' souls are necessarily magnetic, and would tend to dominate, to be the center of any group they participated in. This would make it all the more difficult for that group to realize cooperative leadership. Partly because of this, many of the advanced disciples of the First, Second, and Seventh Ray ashrams stayed with those ashrams and did not become part of the new Synthetic Ashram.

"Yes Mary?"

Mary: "You still haven't said what Lucille means by 'organization'. I've never liked Lucille's use of language, the way she gives common words new meanings, and 'organization' is just one example. The new terminology may work with students of her materials, but what about those who don't have that background?"

Quinn: "Part of the problem with the language is that the original intent appears to have been that students would approach the Wisdom gradually —short, basic introductory lectures followed by short, simple courses, followed by a series of courses of gradually increasing frequency and difficulty, until the student took N.S., and from there could branch out into courses in a number of different service areas. N.S. was meant to be the foundation from which one worked, but was never meant to be the first course one took.

"However, none of that has happened —as of yet— and making it happen is not a particular part of my function.

"The function of the group of which I am a part is much more modest, to model precipitating the Wisdom —NTFPW— into easily accessible popular forms, and this precludes using difficult terminology.[12]

"As for Lucille giving 'organization' a different meaning, I would argue that she didn't, Seventh Ray did that by altering the way things are organized. What R./Lucille did was try to explain that new meaning — and one can hardly begrudge R. a bit of tweaking of the English language, since it appears that he reformulated it into a modern language back around the beginning of the increase of Seventh Ray activity, during his incarnation as Francis Bacon. Which, by the way, may helps explain why English became a predominant world language as Seventh Ray waxed."

Celine: "Makes the tendency of Ceremonial Magicians to use ancient languages and alphabets a bit ironic."

Quinn: "Well, that's a very broad topic, and we really don't have time for it. Basically, it depends on the type of work the language is designed for, and includes such things as structure and sound."

Arista: "Work?"

Quinn: "Well, in our current context 'work' refers to the creative process, either the Magic of Form or the Magic of Consciousness, and how those types of magic are organized.

---

[12] Quinn: Thus, for instance, the conversational tone in *Raising the Queen of Heaven*, with the more throat center material relegated to the back.

Third Ray Organization

Quinn: Of course, we discussed the 'new' Seventh Ray method of working, the Magic of Consciousness, last week. It is a peculiarity of this new magic that one focuses on the creative activity of the consciousness, with no concern for the outer shape or form that result. Again, it's the function of the consciousness to perform the creative, ceremonial magical process, not to create the mental, astral, physical-etheric, or physical-dense forms. Creating the mental, astral, and physical-etheric forms is the function of the devas of those planes, while creating the physical-dense is the function of the elemental.[13]

"Thus, in order to work the Magic of Consciousness properly, a group must perform the inner work without any concern for the outer result.

"Now, we have already discussed the old methods of Seventh Ray, the 'Magic of Form'. But for those of you who were not here, this type of magic is quite ancient, hearkening back to the previous Seventh Ray age in Atlantean times, and one may find examples of it in all human cultures. For instance, a relatively modern example is Freemasonry.

"As we discussed last week, in the ancient 'Magic of Form' systems, the magician used the motion of substance to carry the consciousness and embody the intent. In effect, one created —usually in some sort of ritual— by intentionally identifying with a form, allowing that form to carry one in the direction one wished to go, and then detaching from that form by identifying with another.

"The difficulty with this type of magic is that it's not

---

[13] Glen: See – *The Disciple and Economy*, by Lucille Cedercrans, p. 61

just a Seventh Ray activity, but also a Third Ray process. Because of the identification with and as form, the magical activity was sequential and necessarily had an outer end —a specific result in time and space— in mind from the beginning.

"As a result, the magician was in severe danger of becoming fascinated by, and trapped within their creation.

"So long as the individualized human soul identifies with its forms, and becomes trapped therein, it must experience the death of that form. The cycle of the form carries the trapped consciousness through the birth, maturity, decline, and death of the form. This is an inevitable result of that identification, at *all* planes of human experience —physical-dense, etheric, astral, and mental— and at all levels, from that of individual cells, personas, groups, and entire civilizations."

Zed: "Civilizations?"

Quinn: "Yes, some of the ageless wisdom teachings speak of the cyclic rise and fall of great civilizations, going back in prehistory long before anything archeologists recognize."

Nyle: "Atlantis and Lemuria."

Quinn: Yes, among many others. Now, the reason civilizations rise and fall, the cause behind it, is the identification of the collective consciousness of the civilization with the form of that civilization. It's the exact same mechanism, simply on a larger scale."

Arista: "But, that means that our civilization—"

Quinn: "Can be transformed. Again, keep in mind that what applies to that group which we call an individual human being also applies to larger groups made up of human beings. Thus, if humanity as a whole collectively moves from identifying with and as the form, to identifying with and as the Soul, then the collective form, the entire civilization, will be transformed without the necessity of the death of that form. The Consciousness of humanity will have freed itself from the form of its civilization without the necessity of its death.

"Now, because of these effects of identification with form, groups organized along Third Ray lines are distinguished by several characteristics, including:

"The goal is known from the beginning.

"The goal is defined in numeric terms.

"A domination-based hierarchial structure.

"A cycle of growth, maturity, decline, and death.

"In the Third Ray type of organization, the emphasis of their activities will be on creating, growing, and preserving the physical-dense organization. This would be the case irrespective of the rays of the organization itself.

(Hal became frowny as his throat exuded a lemony light.)

"We see all of these characteristics, for instance, in Freemasonry and in most modern business.

"For instance, in business:

"The goal of a company, at its founding, might be to become 'the number one widget manufacturer in North America', or to become a $100 Billion company by a particular date.

"The structure, goal, and methods of the business would all be laid out from the beginning in a 'business plan'.

"And decisions would be made by a Chief Executive.

"This is a classic, Third Ray organizational structure.

"However, a new type of organization is emerging in this age, one that is built along Seventh Ray lines."

Chapter 2

Seventh Ray Organization

Quinn: "Seventh Ray brings Divine Intent into appearance. In the process, the opposite of that Intent also appears, creating a landing pad, body receptive, or outer condition that leads humanity to invoke the solution to that embodied condition. Thus Seventh Ray tends to produce fairly extreme, conflicting opposites which have to be raised and synthesized into at-one-ment.

"Now, as part of this process, those bringing down the solution often have to embody the difficulty in their own life and affairs, invoke the solution, manifest the solution for themselves, and then model it for humanity —a good example of this would be the founder of Alcoholics Anonymous.

"It should be kept in mind that the first effect of the Energy of Synthesis is to bring polarity into bold relief, preparatory to raising that polarity into a higher condition of at-one-ment or union.

"We are presently seeing this effect of Synthesis throughout humanity's life and affairs, in every field of human activity. The normal reaction of the average human being is to identify with one pole or the other, according to the forms with which they are already identified.

"However, the Disciplic response is to remain identified with and as the consciousness, to find the point of union overshadowing those poles, and to raise those poles —in their consciousness— up into that condition of at-one-ment. The disciple then models that state of consciousness for humanity, which then embodies that union within their life and affairs.

"This is how the Disciplic group practices the Magic of Consciousness in this age, including the way that group is organized.

"In a group life organized along Seventh Ray lines:

"There is no outer goal, or end-point, but a fluid working of the magical process.

"Numerical assessment is largely irrelevant.

"The group structure is organic, based on recognition of the position and function of the group within the greater life, and of the karmic function of each soul within the group. The group expresses this recognition as cooperation, as the cooperation between the various organs of a single body —such as the heart, lungs, kidneys, etc.— each of which supports the other simply by knowing and doing its part.

"The organizational structure of the group remains in the physical-etheric and above, and never descends into or is crystallized in physical-dense form.

"As a result, the Seventh Ray organization is not trapped within the life cycle of substance. There is no 'life span' built into it, because there is no 'life cycle'. Thus, where the life cycle of a Third Ray organization is determined by its form, the precipitation and outer expression of a Seventh Ray organization is determined by the magical process. As a result, when an outer activity of the inner organization has served its purpose, the inner organization simply moves on. Since the outer activity is a moving reflection of the inner magical process, the moment that inner activity moves on, the outer activity ceases, quietly and without struggle, without affecting the inner group work. Put very basically:

"The intent of a group life organized along Third Ray lines will be focused on the outer form.

"The intent of a group life organized along Seventh Ray lines will be focused on working the magical process which manifests purpose.

"This will be the case irrespective of the intent or purpose involved (selfish or Divine), or of the rays of the particular group involved."

Crisis

Quinn: "Now, given the tendency of the Magic of Consciousness to produce polarities in order to resolve them, a Seventh Ray organization always grows through a number of crises. These generally follow the development of the centers or chakras of the group, and the unfoldment of the group life/purpose in each of those centers.

"For instance, if a group were to come together with the intent of invoking and manifesting World Peace, then that intent to manifest peace would have to be worked out and manifested via each of the major and minor centers of the developing group, with each center producing its own crisis of opportunity as that center began to formulate in response to that intent.

"The result will usually be some sort of conflict in the world of affairs, and if the group is unable to hold to their intent despite the conflict, and to manifest that intent because of the conflict, then the group will not survive as such."

Hal: (Radiating the lemony light at Quinn) "The Third Ray type you mentioned must be very advanced, because D.K. says that Third Ray people are so lacking in clarity that they can't communicate clearly, and he suggests they force themselves to speak and write their thoughts clearly, without ambiguity, suggestion, or innuendo." [14]

---

[14] Glen: See – *Glamour, A World Problem*, by Alice A. Bailey, p. 222

Quinn: (Absorbing the lemony light into his fore-head, and radiating a clear, golden-yellow to Hal's aura.) "I was referring to the organizational *structure* of a group, not to the ray makeup of an individual or a group. Such an organization could be First Ray military, Second Ray educational, Fourth Ray artistic, Fifth Ray scientific, Sixth Ray religious, or Seventh Ray ceremonial magic —Freemasons, for instance— and still be organized along Third Ray lines."

Myron: "A moment ago you mentioned the 'centers' of a group or organization. Do you mean group chakras, and was Lucille building such an organization?"

Quinn: "It might help if you think of 'organization' in terms of an 'organism', a Soul life that has been precipitated into the three lower worlds and reflected into time and space. Any such group life will have the same basic structure, whether that life is that of an individualized human being or of an Ashramic Group Unit.

"Keep in mind that in the context of the Seventh Ray type, the term 'organization' has little, well, nothing really, to do with an outer organization or group.

"The basic idea is that the Ashram of Synthesis was being precipitated by seven groups, each of which had its particular place and function within the Ashramic Group Life. One of these was 'The Wisdom Group', which was responsible for precipitating *'The New Thought-form Presentation of the Wisdom'* into the three lower worlds, and into appearance in forms that made that NTFPW available to humanity.

"Now, before that NTFPW could be precipitated by the Wisdom Group into mental energy, astral force, etheric substance, and physical-dense forms, the group itself had to sound its own note into the three lower worlds and build a group instrument that includes group mental, astral, and etheric vehicles. That instrument

Chapter 2

would, in turn, precipitate the Wisdom down to where it could be handed off to a Synthetic Deva of Appearance — which would also have to be built. That Deva of Appearance would in turn call and impress the elementals who would build the outer forms of the new Teaching.

"In order to be vehicles of the NTFPW, all of these group instruments would have to be devas of synthesis. That is, they would be formulated of the Energy of Synthesis and would be functionally a part of the devic life of the Ashram of Synthesis.

"Since no such order of devas existed, the Wisdom Group would have to begin the process by creating that new order.

"When R/Lucille used the term 'organization' in this context, it refers to the devic life of the group, which is synthetic in nature but ordered —if we can use that term— along Seventh Ray lines rather than Third.

"Where a Third Ray organization works toward a preconceived physical goal, assesses it achievements in numeric terms, and is structured as a rigid hierarchy, a Seventh Ray organization focuses on the creative process itself, does not manifest below the physical-etheric, and thus has no crystallized outer structure.

"One of the greatest difficulties that the early group had was figuring out how to do all of the above —creating a Seventh Ray organization with an outer expression. They never managed it, and we're still working on it.

"However, to answer your questions, the 'organization' referred to was the Ashramic Group Unit known in Lucille's materials as 'The Wisdom Group'. The Overshadowing Spiritual Souls of all the members of that little group were and are members or part of that vast Ashramic Unit, but they were only a partial precipitation of it. A great many additional Spiritual Souls were and are equally part of the Group Unit. Some of those were in incarnation back then —I was, for one, although as an infant I had quite a bit of recapitulating to do before I was ready to take up that work in the outer world— and many have come into incarnation since. Of these, many are not and many never become aware of Lucille's works, but this does not affect the fact of their being part of the subjective group life of the organization.

"So, that's it. A Seventh Ray 'organization' is very different from a Third Ray organization, and the absence of a Third Ray type of organization is one of the things that attracted me to the materials."

Angelique: "So, what happened to that organization then, that group work?"

Quinn: "The work continues. The building work is fairly advanced, a lot has been accomplished subjectively, but the physical-dense realm is still resisting it so the bulk of it is not visible here yet. But it's coming."

Angelique: "You're not worried by the delay?"

Quinn: "There's no timetable in Seventh Ray work. Remember, we may appear to be in stage one or two, but Seventh Ray magic is not sequential and can just jump to stage seven. It may be a bit startling to the personas involved, but they adjust."

Zed: "Are there any good examples of group work, and which would you say were the best. What about ...."15

Quinn: "Well, first, from my perspective, the groups you cited are persona based, organized along Third Ray lines, and are motivated by Sixth Ray.

"Remember, in Third Ray organization —the organizational structure of the past age— the end is known from the beginning, that end is seen in terms of a ideal

---

15 Ellora: I omitted the names of three organizations.

56

form which is unfolded in a sequential —1–2–3–4— manner, there is a centralized structure, power flows from that center, and success is evaluated in numerical terms.

"The Sixth Ray motivation of the Third Ray structure directs the efforts of the organization toward achieving an ideal, which may be materialistic or 'spiritual', and which is often embodied in an individual person such as a teacher, guru, or leader.

"When the personas involved are attracted to and organized around a form, whether that of an individual persona, an astral idol or glamour, or a mental ideal, then that group life is orbiting around its persona and is a persona based group.

"That type of organization often takes on an outer, physical-dense form and its members then identify and thereby become trapped in that group form. Now, we'll be discussing group work next week, but I can say a few words here.

"At this point, a group disciple is a unit of consciousness within an Ashram, identified with a portion of the Ashramic Purpose, which bears the responsibility for manifesting that fragment of the Ashramic Purpose. In this age, such a group will be organized along Seventh Ray lines, will be identified as a group consciousness which is focused on precipitating its Divine Intent, and will not necessarily have a recognizable outer group structure.

"Seventh Ray work is cyclic, but not sequential. That is, the Magic of Consciousness can move from 1 to 4 without going through the intervening steps of 2 & 3. Thus, among other things, groups of this type do not evaluate their efforts numerically but instead align the responding substance back up with the overshadowing Intent.

"In addition, since the group is identified with and as the magical work of consciousness, rather than the form, the consciousness of the group does not identify with and become trapped in the form. As a result, the form itself does not crystallize but remains fluid, responsive to the precipitating intent. Without crystallization, there is no outer physical-dense organization to point to and identify. The group life does not manifest, as such, below the physical-etheric.

"To answer your immediate question, I have no particular thoughts on what the best examples of real group work might be. I am familiar with several examples of Ashramic Group Units which have and are precipitating their ashramic group life into the three lower worlds, and reflecting that into the world of affairs. But, by their nature they are not something that can be easily identified or pointed to in the physical-dense.

"In addition, during the first seven seven-year cycles, the Group Units of the Synthesis Ashram were primarily focused on the Seventh Ray inner building work, precipitating the substantial life of the Group Units into the three lower worlds. As a result, their service work was somewhat muted or hidden by the building work, making the groups very difficult to see."

Masters

Mary: "Earlier you mentioned idealizing gurus. One of my teachers belonged to the Esoteric Section of the T.S. when she was young, and back then they had picture of the Masters on the walls of their lodge, and she got so tired of the veneration, like they were saints or something, that she left the Society. That was obviously Sixth Ray aspiration to a persona, which Master's don't have. But this 'New Presentation of the Wisdom', it's not under the guidance of just one master, or even three, really, but, what, a 'Monad of Synthesis? This feels very close to an inner truth I've long felt but was confused about."

Chapter 2

Quinn: "Umm... That gets into a number of things. We'll discuss the 'Monad of Synthesis' in two weeks, in the workshop on the Ashram. The Sixth Ray veneration of personas will gradually pass away as we move into the Seventh Ray.[16] However, that veneration will be with us for some time to come! Certainly the majority of us —humanity— who were raised from their infancy to venerate spiritual figures such as Jesus, Buddha, etc., will take those glamours to the grave with us. The incoming Seventh Ray is relieving those glamours, but largely through conflict."

Hugh: "Isn't that Fourth Ray?"

Quinn: "No, that's 'Harmony through Conflict'. Seventh is 'Order through Conflict'".

(Myron's tummy went rumbly —a dissonant E-flat oozing orangish fog. Quinn added a lavender hue to the light radiating to the group.)

Zed: "What? Where's that written?"

Quinn: "I don't know that it is. You just have to observe Seventh in action to realize that it works that way. Remember, the energy of Synthesis stimulates the pairs of opposites into expression, creating the opportunity to bring them into union or at-one-ment in Divine Law and Order. One way of describing that process is 'Order through Conflict'. It's what the Magic of Consciousness does."

Arista: "What I'm wondering is how we start planning for that kind of future, of organized group work. How do we use our energies to move in the right direction?"

Quinn: "Well, that's just it. Under the Seventh Ray way of working, one doesn't 'plan', one manifests The Plan. One ascends in meditation to at-one with that portion of the Ashramic Plan which is the life of one's

---

16 Quinn: See also the guru-chela relationship as discussed in Chapter 3.

Ashramic Group, and then descends with that fragment of The Plan, transforming it into energy, force, and substance, and projecting that onto the reflecting surface of the physical-dense realm, and then relating that back up to the source and repeating the cycle.

(Quinn repeated the process of building the indigo-white cone of light —upward from the cave to the overshadowing, 'silently' sounding an A-natural chorus down and out to the group aura, and F-natural up from there out of *sight*— reflecting that process in his words.)

"It's not planning, it's, well, planting. Only, unlike with gardening, you're usually quite surprised at the result because it's not something you planned for or expected from the start."

(Myron's aura started bubbling like a koi pond at feeding time as little forms surfaced and demanded attention.)

Myron: "We have to keep in mind the goal of at-one-ment! The appearance of union is easy, you simply avoid conflicts. But true at-one-ment is achieved via Harmony through Conflict. That can be a bitter pill, but those are often the most effective."

Quinn: "Well, not really. The Seventh Ray worker doesn't avoid conflict. They perform the creative process, the Magic of Consciousness, realizing that it will produce the *appearance* of conflict, but that that appearance will be resolved, via Magic, into Order.

(Myron's belly and throat wigged out. His aura boiled for a moment, and then spewed dark wriggly things. Quinn's brow reached out with indigo-gold, caught, and absorbed them, darkening and churning his aura in turn, but the indigo-white light in the cave remained clean and bright.)

"I was referring to separation and union as states of consciousness, not conditions of the form. In that context, union requires the at-one-ment of consciousness with consciousness. The method by which this is achieved will vary somewhat from one Ray makeup to another.

(The wriggly things squirmed frantically amidst the higher vibrations of Quinn's aura, fleeing towards it edges but being pulled back in.)

"Also, in the current Seventh Ray planetary age, the emphasis is moving from 'ascending to at-one-ment' to realizing union by manifesting it through Ceremonial Magic —the Ceremonial Magic of Consciousness. In this context, the Ray of union is Seventh —*Order* Through Conflict— rather than Fourth —Harmony Through Conflict."

(Myron grabbed his notebook, stood, and stormed out. The group watched him leave with a mixture of concern and relief. Zed turned from watching him leave, glanced at his wrist, and tapped it to draw Quinn's attention to the time.)

Hugh: "One final point, when a Disciplic group does manifest in time and space, what's the best outer form, a non-profit or what?"

(Twitching at a higher and higher pace, the things shattered and dissolved. Quinn's spinning aura caught up the remnants and sucked them downward into the Earth.)

Quinn: "Well, that is an important point. The basic answer is that a Group Unit that precipitates its Ashramic Life via the Magic of Consciousness does not and cannot manifest in *a* legal structure. Now, this is crucial. Remember, the Ashramic Group Unit precipitates its place and function into the three lower worlds, thereby manifesting its portion of the Ashram in the mental, astral, and physical-etheric. However, that is an ongoing creative process. It doesn't stop, but continues to evolve with the group as the group practices the magical process. So there's no end-point, no final goal as far as precipitating the group is concerned. It's a magical process.

"However, while that Group Life must be reflected in turn into the physical-dense, that reflection is a reflection of a moving picture of the Ashramic Life, and the physical-dense is like a snapshot, a fixed image. Thus, the moment one identifies an outer structure, any outer structure, as being the outer expression of the inner Group, you interfere with that magical motion, that moving picture.

"Basically, any fixed image, whether that's an organizational structure or an idea of what a group should do, will interfere with the magical creative process. This includes everything from formal business plans to, well, showing up at group meetings with a set idea of what the group is supposed to do.

"So, since one must create outer forms to embody some aspects of the Group Life —to open bank accounts, rent meeting space, etc.— one recognizes that all such outer, legal organizations are merely temporary clothing, packaging that enables the group to interact with its body receptive and with humanity.

"Any more questions?

"OK, we'll close in the usual fashion."

Chapter 2

Closing Meditation

Quinn: "As a group, renew the upward line of indigo-white light from the group ajna, through the group crown center, to the Wisdom and that portion of the Wisdom overshadowing the group. (pause)

"As a group in the ajna, invoke that portion of the Wisdom downward, through the three lower worlds and into the group brain awareness, by audibly sounding the OM. (long pause)

"From the ajna, project that Wisdom outward into appearance in the group life and affairs by again audibly sounding the OM. (long pause)

"From the ajna, align the group brain upward, via a line of indigo-white light, back up to the overshadowing Wisdom. Again, audibly sound the OM. (pause)

"Leaving the alignment in place, slowly relax the attention and return to this here and now."

Postscript

I woke after we exited the freeway, as we rolled to a stop at the first light. He hadn't spoken at all since the closing meditation. His aura still looked pallid, but not as raggedy as before, and he was coming back from wherever he'd been. As we drove, I watched the light in his head expand as its notes dropped through a series of octaves. Finally, as we neared home, he moved out to his brow and was back.

"Is it like that often?", I asked.

His brow center cleared and tightened, just a bit, and he said, "It's the magic. Makes the polarities plain, clear, and then lifts them into union."

"But you go through all that."

"You have to lead the group into, through it."

As we turned into our cul-de-sac, his brow wavered, then lost its clarity as we pulled into our drive and stopped. Home, he set the brake, and said, "Umm... Sorry, but I'm done. We'll finish tomorrow."

"Would you like tea or something?"

"Too tired. Straight to bed."

I called in his own guardian then, and Max came and we watched over him all through the rest of the night.

Chapter 3

Group Discipleship

Zed's smile began and ended at his mouth. There was a gap at the place at the table where Myron usually sat, and Hal looked really scowley. The group aura swirled as Zed waved us into the room and toward our chairs. Amanda's eyes crinkled as she opened her arms, and I trotted into her embrace. By the time she released me all the women were smiling at us, most of the men were holding back grins, and much of the remaining tension was dissipating.

Quinn had silently found his seat and begun composing the indigo-white alignment. I shed my pack and began setting things up. Quinn closed his eyes, and completed the indigo-white triangle while I worked.

The room grew quiet and still, and with everything set, I turned on the recorder.

Opening Alignment

Move up into the ajna center and integrate the three-fold persona into a single unit.

From the ajna, align upward via a line of indigo-white through the crown center to and with that portion of the Wisdom which overshadows Group Discipleship.

From the ajna, invoke that portion of the Wisdom related to Group Discipleship downward into appearance by audibly sounding the OM. (long pause)

From the ajna, project that Wisdom outward to the group brain awareness by again audibly sounding the OM.

From the ajna, align the group brain upward, via a line of indigo-white light, directly to the overshadowing Wisdom. Again, audibly sound the OM. (pause)

Leaving this triangular alignment in place, slowly relax the attention and return to your normal focus.

Chapter 3

Group Discipleship

Quinn: "Well, it's nice to see some younger faces tonight. Has everyone heard the tapes? Yes? OK.[17]

"This evening's subject is 'Group Discipleship', which is closely related to Group Initiation. The primary distinction being that where initiation is a stage of the *evolution* of consciousness, discipleship is the *function* of the consciousness during that stage. You could say that where initiation is a state of consciousness, discipleship is the activity of consciousness while in that state.

"Now, our conversation tonight will probably include both that state of consciousness which is the New Path of Group Initiation and that activity which is Group Discipleship.

"Of course, with this group I don't need to explain either the old path of initiation or discipleship, but we'll probably touch on them as well.

"Now, that leaves the question, 'What is a group disciple?'

"A group disciple is a self-identified unit of consciousness within the Ashram. That ashramic group unit consists of Spiritual Souls who, in a sense, share the same purpose, a 'portion' of the ashramic purpose, which is itself a portion of the Divine Plan."

Angelique: "Like the purpose of the Synthetic Ashram."

Quinn: "Yes.

"That unit of group consciousness, with a spark of ashramic purpose at its heart, is united by a complex web of ashramic substance.

"Thus, an ashramic group unit is, within the ashram, one in purpose, consciousness, and substance. In other

---

[17] Ellora: I've omitted occasional questions and comments by new students about previous workshops.

words, it is a single life consisting of multiple lives.

"The central, motivating impulse of the group life is its purpose, and that purpose is the life of the group. It inspires the group members and attracts those who need what the group offers."

Hal: "The members who need the purpose?"

Quinn: "Umm, no. The group purpose, radiated by its consciousness and carried out and down by its devic life, attracts the body receptive, those whom the group serves by fulfilling its purpose.

"In order to fulfill its purpose and function within the ashram that group unit precipitates itself downward into the three lower worlds, and in turn into time and space. At first, its appearance is as multiple apparently-unrelated personas. However, as those personas grow in consciousness, they slowly become aware of themselves as Soul. As they become aware of themselves as Soul, they become aware of their overshadowing Soul life — their place, function, and activity as a part of an ash-ramic group unit— and the place and function of that unit within the greater ashramic life.

"From this perspective, the personae of a Spiritual Soul are part of the instrument of the ashramic group unit, and any pattern or condition in any one of those personas exists in the instrument of the group. This must be the case, for they are all part of the same life, whether they are aware of it in time and space or not."

Hal: "Is that the same as the groups described in Rule Eleven."[18]

---

[18] Quinn: Probably "Rule XI" in *The Rays and The Initiations*, by Alice A. Bailey, pp. 22-23. "For Disciples and Initiates: Let the group together move the fire within the Jewel in the Lotus into the Triad and let them find the Word which will carry out that task. Let them destroy by their dynamic Will that

Chapter 3

Quinn: "Most of A.A.B.'s works were written before the reformulation of my Ashram —the Ashram of Synthesis. That Ashram of necessity functions somewhat differently from those she describes, and has a peculiar responsibility for and has been actively developing the process of group initiation. However, D.K. was one of the co-creators of the new Ashram, and the senior *disciples* involved prepared for the new work for several incarnations. So, D.K. must at least have anticipated the work of the new ashram, even if there was no way to know exactly what the new path would look like until the disciples involved formulated it."

Arista: "The disciples? Wouldn't the Masters have done that?"

Quinn: "Umm... This touches a bit on next week. Basically, the three Masters at the heart of the Synthetic Ashram hold its overall focus of Purpose, and radiate that Purpose throughout the Group Life of the Ashram. But, it's the function of that Group Life to precipitate that Purpose into the three lower worlds. In the process, as that Group Life —all the group units together— precipitate the Ashramic Plan, they formulate the New Path of Group Initiation. We create the New Path of Initiation as we walk it.

"Given this, it's somewhat difficult to determine to what degree D.K.s descriptions of group disciples applies to the Synthesis Ashram and to the current process of group initiation.

"Also, while Bailey and Cedercrans provide some useful guidelines, workers in the Synthesis Ashram tend to

---

which has been created at the midway point. When the point of tension is reached by the brothers at the fourth great cycle of attainment, then will this work be done." The rule is explained on pp. 208 - 225 prefer —because of the nature of that Ashram— to focus on participating in the inner work *of* the Ashram.

"And regarding the 'Laws of Initiation', it may help if we look at the path as being in some ways like a living, growing, organism, slowly transforming over time.

"The path as described in our spiritual traditions and modeled for us by initiates of the past ages is that of the 'perfected man', the individual who has achieved immortality via transcendence of the form.

"In the New Path of Group Initiation the goal is telepathic at-one-ment of the group unit, and the precipitation of that group consciousness throughout its entire life and affairs.

"The path ahead is Soul Realization, by the entire human kingdom, at all levels of its existence. When that occurs, every human being —at whatever level of growth and development, and wherever they are in the Wheel of Life— will be aware that they *are* Soul.

"That is a basic description of the path of initiation as expressed in the past, present, and future. As always, it's the same path, yet, as always, it's different for every individual, in every society, and at every level of human growth and development.

"Now, a comparison of the 'Laws of Initiation' as expressed in the 'old' path and the 'new' would be a course in itself, and would require a focused, consistent and persistent group effort to precipitate, and that's not our goal this evening. However, I would suggest that what has changed is not the basic 'Laws' governing the path, but humanity's approach to and experience of the path due to the growth and development of human consciousness.

"For instance, for Atlantean humanity —which had not yet developed the concrete rational mind— the path was almost purely mystical and did not have the more

70

recent occult elements. For intellectual Aryan humanity the primary focus was on the mental side of the path, and the current methods include in their foundations a synthesis of the mystical and the occult.

"Details of the New Path of Group Initiation are included in some of the works published by Wisdom Impressions, such as *Ashramic Projections*, and *Leadership Training*, and the upcoming *Applied Wisdom*. However, much remains overshadowing, in the *New Thought-form Presentation of the Wisdom*, and has yet to be precipitated.

"Some of what I've said about Group Initiation will also be in my upcoming class, *Raising the Queen of Heaven*, and more will be in the following courses on *The Magic of Consciousness*. However, those will be formulated for a broad portion of humanity, and will not have the same... abstract intensity... as Lucille's works."

(Hal's aura swirled with redish flashes, especially around his throat.)

Hal: "But this is the time of individualization. The direction of the human development for hundreds of years and into this age is toward awakening the individual, and the focus should be on *the Soul's* realization of Christ Consciousness."

Quinn: "Well, a couple points. First, in order to move into Group Consciousness, to become aware of and take up one's place and function as a Group Disciple, one's individual identity must be strong enough that it will not be threatened by the prospect.

"There's a common misconception that the individual self is lost or dissipated as one develops group awareness. However, in a sense the reverse is the case. You have to have a strong enough self-awareness that you can become group aware without losing your self in the process. Otherwise, the moment you *try* to become group aware, your individual self will —quite properly— feel that its very existence is threatened and will do everything it can to assert itself and block the development of group awareness. It's a difficult transition in any case, and many of the difficulties of the aspirant to group discipleship are due to this sort of resistance.

"Amanda?"

Amanda: "So, one has to become a strong, integrated, fully-developed individual in order to become group conscious."

Quinn: "Yes."

"Now, the next point is the question of what is meant by 'individualization' in this context.

"From my perspective, although it's still very early in the age, it is more of an age of *group* initiation —a process in which the individualized identity of Ashramic Group Units precipitate their selves, and their ashramic activity, into the world of affairs.

"This is part of a larger process which will continue through 'individualization' of group units, to entire Ashrams, and eventually of the Christ.

"Thus, one has the *eventual* 'individualization' of:

"Members of the animal kingdom.

"A human persona, via the synthesis of its various parts —bodies, thought-forms, etc.

"An Ashramic Group Unit —an organ or group life within an Ashram— via the synthesis of their collective Soul and personae.

"An Ashram, via the synthesis of its Group Units.

"The Christ or World Teacher, via the synthesis of:
  "humanity —integrated personas,
  "the world discipleship —Ashramic Group Units— and,

72

Chapter 3

"the Hierarchy —Ashramic Group Lives,
"into a one consciousness.

"The human kingdom is preparing for the greatest
expansion of consciousness since individualization. At
the end of the age we will have an opportunity to take
initiation *as a kingdom*. At that point, each and every
member of the human kingdom will be aware —from
whatever their individual level of development— that
they are Soul. At present, of course, this level of Soul
identification is a characteristic of those who have
evolved beyond the human identification into that of the
Spiritual Kingdom. However, when the human kingdom
takes that initiation, what had been a characteristic of
the 'Kingdom of Conscious Souls' will become a characteristic of the human kingdom.

"But keep in mind that we are part of a planetary
life. One kingdom cannot grow and develop without the
others doing so as well, and helping the lower kingdoms
evolve in consciousness, all of the lower kingdoms, is
part of the task of the world discipleship. Thus, as we
move up into our higher, proper place and function, so
will the mineral, plant, and animal kingdoms."

Angelique: "I read an interesting article recently in-
forming parents about 'indigo children', and it seems to
me that it was of good example of how we should be
manifesting the Wisdom, working in our immediate
family and community and beginning the change there."

Quinn: "Yes. That's a very good point, and in our current context I'd add this. In the New Path of Initiation
there won't necessarily be any particularly distinctive
features in the incarnating members of a Group Disciple, none that cry out 'here is an initiate'. The members
of such a group will most likely appear quite ordinary in
their childhood and youth, if a bit more focused than

average. For them, having a powerfully-demanding individual ego is a disadvantage. They need an ego that is so self-assured that it does not need to be the center of attention, and will not be threatened by the process of at-oneing with the Group. Thus, the tendency of self-assertion that one finds in less self-assured personas is muted, and it isn't until the group comes together that one has the appearance of Disciplic Consciousness in time and space.

(Hal's belly aura began rippling with streaks of sandy bits.)

"However, once the Group appears, each member of that group life carries that consciousness with them and embodies it in their life and affairs —as a part of the group life and affairs."

(The ripples became waves that washed into his aura and isolated the brighter points of light like the ramparts of a sand castle.)

Hal: "Wouldn't more advanced Souls progress more rapidly on their own? There'd always be those who lag behind, retarding the progress of the group. So if we were on our own..."

(Sounding a silent F-Sharp, pure green radiated from Quinn's brow toward Hal's heart.)

Quinn: "With respect, this is rather like suggesting that the hands retard the progress of the feet.

(Hal's points of light held, but the sandy waters flashed outward toward Quinn.)

"A group disciple is a single consciousness, a group soul, and functions as such as a unit within the Ashram. Portions of that group unit may appear to progress at different rates in the three lower worlds. However, the entire unit is precipitating itself, into the three lower worlds and into time and space, as a one life, and each portion of that life has its particular role in the process.

74

Chapter 3

"When viewed in this perspective, the apparent levels of growth and development of individual personas are simply part of the process, and taken as a whole, the process of group initiation is much more rapid than that which might be called individual initiation, as the new process enables the group to achieve in a few incarnations what formerly took individuals hundreds or thousands.

"In this context, the 'imperfections' in a group disciple's persona represents the scope of its service. Basically, in order to embody the solution for a pattern of difficulty, a group disciple will incarnate with that pattern of difficulty, and, in discovering the solution to that problem for itself, build a pattern of solution for humanity. The classic example of this is the story of the founder of Alcoholics Anonymous.

(Still holding the group alignment, Quinn's aura met the assaulting waters with indigo light, and absorbed them.)

"The corollary of this principle is also true. If a group separates itself from those with a certain pattern of difficulty —illusion, glamour, maya, or outer dis-ease— then they cut themselves off from those with that condition. That group will not then be able to relate the overshadowing solution to the embodied need, or the embodied need with the overshadowing solution.

(The sandy waters spun into Quinn's central lines of light, up, out and down in a twirling fountain, and were sucked in and up again.)

"Thus, a group disciple cannot limit its associates or members to those free of illusion, glamour, maya, or disease, for were it to do so it would drive off all of its potential associates and members, separate itself from those whom it aspired to serve, and disrupt its ability to perform subjective service.

(In and up and out and down the waters spun, and the bits cleared, softened, and joined the light.)

"The work is done by those who show up. They will bring illusions and glamours with them, but those distortions are part of the group, part of its area of service, and they will be transmuted and adjusted as part of the group service. Those who are too attached to their distortions to change will leave, those who can transform will continue with the work, and the group work will continue."

(Quinn's aura radiated clear yellow-gold to Hal, returning the purified waters.)

Nyle: "What about ray glamours? Wouldn't the members of these groups have the same Soul Ray and the same basic ray glamours, and doesn't that amount to, well, separating out glamours of other rays?"

Quinn: "Well, sort of, but not quite. Keep in mind that the Group Unit is a being in itself. The Group has its Purpose and Life, Consciousness or Soul, and Substance or Intelligent Activity. Each of these Group Aspects has its own ray makeup, and that ray makeup is part of the character and quality of the Group, just as our own makeup is part of each of us."

Arista: "But the Group Soul and Substance is just a collection of human souls and personas."

Quinn: "From an individual human perspective, yes. However, from the perspective of the Ashramic Group Unit it's the other way around. When you enter into meditation, align with, move into, and identify as your Ashramic Group Unit, you are a single 'I'dentity'. An I'dentity or Soul that has its motivating Purpose and formulating Substance, and from *its* perspective:

"The Purpose of each Soul in the Group is *part of* the Purpose of the Group.

76

Chapter 3

"Each individualized Soul in the Group is *part of* the Soul of the Group.

"The Substance of each Soul in the Group is *part of* the Substance of the Group.

"It's equivalent to your heart center recognizing that, while it has its purpose, consciousness, and substance, it's a related part of a larger group life, of an individualized human soul.

"Now, as you become aware of the Purpose, Consciousness, and Substance of the Group Unit, you also become aware of the ray qualities of the Group as *your* rays!"

Arista: "But D.K. applies only six rays to individuals."

Quinn: "Exactly! A Group Unit is another type, another level of individual, and it has its own ray makeup, just as we do. One could say:

"From the Sixth Ray 'ascent' perspective, each Soul in a Group Unit ascends to at-one-ment or union with the Group.

"From the Seventh Ray 'descent' perspective, the Group Unit precipitates itself as fragments of consciousness, and associated mental, astral, and physical-etheric substance.

"Thus, when we approach the subject of ray makeup *as* a Group Disciple we find:

"The Group Monadic Ray is that of the monad at the heart of the Ashram.

"The Group Soul Ray is that of the Purpose of the Group Unit.

"The Group Persona Ray is that of the overall group instrument within the Ashramic Group Life.

"The subrays of the group instrument —mental, astral,

and physical-etheric— will vary from group incarnation to group incarnation, and will depend on the portion of the group purpose and function that is being precipitated into that plane at that point.

"Of course, none of this changes our own, individual ray makeups. It merely expands our awareness of the constellation of rays in which we function.

"To answer your earlier question Nyle, just as we each have our own pattern of illusions, glamours, and maya, so does each Group Unit, and in a sense our individual distortions are every bit a part of that of the Group's as is our purpose and consciousness.

"Since the Group Life is organized along Seventh Ray lines, the group instrument, including its distortions, is precipitated into incarnation in the three lower worlds via the magical process as needed.

"Also, the group instrument is not reflected in time and space as a single entity. The physical-dense instruments of individual members are aligned with the group vertically, but are not integrated horizontally. Thus, there is no group ray in a physical-dense sense."

Zed: "So, a Seventh Ray group is leaderless, deathless, and the antithesis of the old Sixth Ray modus operandi?"

Quinn: "Well, I realize I'm being picky here, however, while a Seventh Ray organization does not have an individual leader, it is not 'leaderless'. The old hologram analogy is useful here —every fragment includes the whole. Just as:

"Each Ashram is responsible for its portion of the Divine Plan,

"every Group Unit within that ashram is responsible for its fragment of the ashramic plan, and

"each disciple within the Group Unit is responsible for their portion of the group unit plan.

Chapter 3

"Thus, each disciple in an Ashramic Group Unit is responsible for focusing and precipitating their portion of the group plan —in coordination with and as an identified part of the whole— and is, as a result, in a position of 'leadership'.

"So, in a Seventh Ray organization every member is a leader. Naturally, the initial result —during a group's transition from the Sixth Ray approach to Third Ray organizations, to the new type of organization— is chaos, until the various externalizations of the group unit learn to recognize and accommodate each other's place and function within the whole. In effect, a Seventh Ray organization cannot function until its members reach and manifest group awareness and intelligent activity, and that awareness and activity is achieved by, well, just by doing the inner work and outer activity.

"Also, and this is a very important point, the new Seventh Ray structure does not in any way invalidate the old Third Ray type of organization. What the Seventh Ray structure gives us is an *additional* method of precipitating the work. The Third Ray organizational structure remains a crucial part of our civilization, and will into the indefinite future."

Mary: "What about Sixth Ray idealism? Does it have a place in Group Initiation?"

Quinn: "While Sixth Ray is waning and its forms are passing away, it still plays a vital role. In the Magic of Consciousness, for instance, the Sixth Ray ascent enables us to focus on the overshadowing purpose, ashramic life, idea, etc., which we are working to manifest in the more Seventh Ray precipitation.

"The Current difficulty with Sixth Ray was formerly one of its prime benefits.

"For instance, in the old Piscean systems the chela who could not *Ascend* —Sixth Ray motion— sufficiently to see or experience the Divine could experience the Divine indirectly via a relationship with a guru who could at-one with the Divine. A western example of this is seen in the Grail romances, in which two knights reach the Grail Castle. While only one of them manages to 'see' the Grail, the other observes the first 'seeing' the Grail. Subjectively, the alignment involved is:

"From the Guru's perspective: Up to the Divine, and out from the guru to the chela, and back from the chela through the guru.

"From the Chela's perspective: To the guru, and through the guru to the Divine.

"Functionally, the chela literally sees the divine in and through the guru. This type of alignment worked fine in the Age of Devotion, and when chela's were required to maintain a very pure lifestyle. However, problems are bound to arise when this alignment is used with modern students who are subject to all the stresses and impurities of modern life. This is because in this alignment the students are functionally a part of the persona of the guru in a very direct way. So much so that any impurities in the student group are conveyed to the guru, producing difficulties in the guru which are conveyed in turn to the students, which are in turn... Well, eventually it leads to a breakdown in the higher alignment of the guru.

"Unfortunately, as the upper alignment breaks down, the guru's persona turns increasingly to and becomes dependent on the group persona of the chelas. The mental energy and astral force of the chelas, focused on the guru, enable his persona to maintain a semblance of the old alignment and magnetism. However, it is a semblance only. The guru's magnetism slowly wanes, and the guru falls into a downward spiral that leads to the sort of tragedies with which we have become all too familiar. Such do not necessarily invalidate the guru's original teachings, but they do indicate part of the difficulty with the old way of doing things in the new context.

"In this age, Teachers working along Seventh Ray lines use a somewhat different alignment that avoids these difficulties:

"As the Teaching Group, the teacher aligns upward —from the cave in the center of the head— with the Teaching, Ashramic Life, Plan, etc.,

"outward through the ajna to the Student Group, and

"upward from the Student Group directly to the Teaching —without going through or even touching the Teacher's instrumentality during this ascent.

"In effect, the Teacher builds a direct alignment between the student group —including all of its members— and the teaching, giving the students direct access. Thus, the students will tend to direct their attention to the *Teaching*, and not to the persona of the Teacher, avoiding most of the difficulties of the old method.

"Of course, the waxing Seventh Ray is stimulating some of the old expressions —and polarities— of the Sixth. This produces, among many other things, an attempt to approach the Synthetic Ashram via the old Sixth Ray methods. These attempts are usually quite astral, heavily englamoured, and emphasize 'Ascension' rather than precipitation or manifestation."

Angelique: "I don't see how this kind of group can register and interpret its Ashramic purpose. How do they come to a consensus about what their purpose is, and respond to that. I realize this is part of what they must learn, but it sounds like the whole attunement/manifestation process would be based on trial and error, qualified by Divine Law and Order."

Quinn: "The N.S. technique? Yes, using that would be a very good idea.[19]

"These are excellent questions, but it really takes a group service project to answer them, one in which one participates in manifesting the life and work of an Ashramic Group Unit. The preparation for such an effort could easily require a series of experiential courses, and *The Nature of the Soul* was originally intended to be a foundation for such a program.

"However, I will attempt brief responses to some of your questions.

"A group's ability to 'register', 'interpret', and 'respond' are functions of its Divine Intelligence or Substantial Aspect. In order to do any and all of these well, the physical, astral, and mental instruments need to be transmuted to the point where they are sensitive and responsive to higher impression, and integrated into a single instrument.

"In order for the group to achieve this purification and integration, the individual members must be well on the way to achieving it.

"However, while purification and integration is a necessary effect on the collective instrument, it is not the goal of the group consciousness. The collective consciousness will be holding the alignment between its overshadowing intent or Ashramic Group Purpose and the group instrument, outward to the body receptive of that intent —that portion of the greater life whom the

---

[19] Quinn: *The Nature of the Soul*, p. 266, "If this be according to Divine Intent, then let it manifest in Divine Law and Order."

group serves— and aligning or relating that body recep-tive back upward to the intent or solution to their em-bodied need.

"Now the practical realization of all of this does, as you suggest, take a certain amount of cooperative at-tempts and trial and error, a great deal of error, requir-ing a large amount of mutual trust and tolerance.

"The group task is perhaps easier to undertake when one has an enunciated purpose to align with from the beginning or inception of the outer group. 'We're going to align with and precipitate our Ashramic Group Pur-pose' is a bit vague to be particularly magnetic, and it assumes that the personnel participating in that effort are part of the same Ashramic Group Unit and thus have a shared purpose —which is not necessarily the case when they are drawn together by something other than the clear broadcast of that purpose.

"However, if one begins with a clear statement of in-tent, such as 'Our purpose is to invoke the Soul of Amer-ica', then one begins with a magnetic focus of intent which will attract those related to that intent, hold them in relationship, and radiate outward to its body receptive."

Arista: "But if each of us is focused on our fragment of the group purpose, and each group is aligned with its fragment of the ashramic purpose, how do we cooperate? Everyone's focused on their own little piece!"

Quinn: "Well, when you're identified with and as the Group, you see everything from the perspective of the Group Consciousness. You see in consciousness how every part of the group is related to every other part, as a one life, and you see how the Group Unit is related to every other Ashramic Group Unit as part of the Ash-ramic Group Life. Thus, you experience your individual purpose only as a part of the Group Purpose, and the

Group Purpose as part of the Ashramic Purpose.

"Since you see and experience your purpose and consciousness as part of the larger whole, your actions follow suit and you naturally work in cooperation with your coworkers.

"The seeds of this ability to work cooperatively within a larger life are developed as we integrate the persona in the ajna center, and it matures as we build a cave center.[20]

"Now, although the cave is commonly associated with a physical location in the body —the center of the head— and with a frequency of energy, the cave center is actually that state of consciousness in which the Overshadowing Spiritual Soul, the human soul, and the animal soul are synthesized into *The Soul*.

"The Soul is group conscious, and from that perspective one perceives or rather experiences the group intent at the heart of The Soul.

"Since it is the nature of consciousness to relate, that Divine Intent of the Soul is radiated by the group consciousness to its persona in the three lower worlds, which interprets that intent into mental, astral, and physical-etheric substance, and the persona in turn projects that energy, force, and substance onto the reflecting surface of the physical-dense.

"Since it is the nature of Substance to differentiate, the form differentiates that purpose or intent into many interpretations. Those identified with the form will perceive the original intent less clearly, if at all, and will identify with one of its forms of expression —often rejecting other forms as incorrect.

---

[20] Glen: See – *Creative Thinking, The Soul and Its Instrument* (for persona integration), and *The Nature of the Soul*, by Lucille Cedercrans

Chapter 3

"Those identified as the Group Consciousness in the cave will remain focused on the overshadowing Purpose or Intent throughout the precipitation process. They will recognize the resulting ideas, thoughts, feelings, etc., as partial expressions of that intent, and collect those expressions in order to achieve a more complete understanding, but will not identify with any of them.

"So, that's basically it. You become the Soul in the Ashram. There you discover your Ashramic Group Life and the Purpose at the heart of that group life, and take up your magical work, as a group, of precipitating your portion of that purpose into appearance."

(The group aura continued to clear and sharpen.)

Kelley: "What happens if a group becomes, well, attached to its work?"

Quinn: "To the outer result? A couple things. First, there are a number of crises in the life of any group endeavor. These generally follow the development of the chakras of the group, and the unfoldment of the group life/purpose in each of those centers.

"For instance, if a group were to come together with the intent of invoking and manifesting World Peace, then that intent to manifest peace would have to be worked out and manifested, via each major and minor center of the developing group, with each center producing its own crisis of opportunity as that center began to develop in response to that intent.

"The result will usually be some sort of conflict in the world of affairs, and if the group is unable to hold to their intent despite the conflict, and to manifest that intent because of that conflict, then the group will not survive as such."

Ellee: "What about creating an educational program for children?"

Quinn: "Now, what I'm about to say may not make

much sense to many of you, yet, but it is something you already know on soul levels.

"The Group Life of the Synthesis Ashram consists of a number of Group Units or Group Disciples each of which has a place and function within that Ashram.

"Each Group Unit is a magical formulation of the three aspects of the Ashram, or of purpose, consciousness, and intelligence. Within the Group Unit those three aspects are formulated into Group Centers —a group Crown Center, Synthetic or Cave Center, Ajna Center, Throat Center, and Heart Center.

"Each of those centers consists of a formulation of the three aspects of that center —a Center Nucleus, Center Petals, and Center Aura.

"The Center Nucleus holds the primary responsibility for the function of that center within the Group Unit.

"Each of the Center Petals is responsible for precipitating a portion of that center function in a particular formulation.

"The aura of each petal —a portion of the aura of the center— is responsible for relating that petal to its body receptive."

Hal: "Would the number of petals be the same as in an individual's centers?"

Quinn: "Well, I'm not really the one to ask. There is a correspondence in the functions of the centers, but the number of petals would be determined by the note of motivating purpose sounding within the group and in the centers within that group. So I'd be very cautious about trying to equate, for instance, the number of petals in a Group Unit's heart center with the number of petals in an individual's heart center. Although their function is similar, their motivating purpose may be quite different.

Chapter 3

"You see, the primary difference between a Second and Seventh Ray description of such things would be that the Second Ray approach tends to describe the center, 'this is what it is and what it does' —those on Second tend to describe the relationships of something to everything else— while the Seventh Ray approach tends to describe how to use it, 'go here and do this' — those on the Seventh tend to model how to manifest Divine Intent via the Magic of Consciousness. So, because of my place and function, I'm not particularly concerned with things like the number of group units in an ashram, or with detailed descriptions of a center.

"Now, all of these functions are interrelated in an organic sense. That is, none exists, none can exist apart from the others —any more than a finger exists apart from its hand.

"Now, as I've mentioned to some of you, my function within the Wisdom Group is within the Group Heart Center, as part of the Nucleus of that Center. Like any center, the Group Heart Center has a number of petals —in various stages of manifestation. Each of those heart center petals has a function within that of the Heart Center, including petals responsible for healing, teaching, etc.

"For instance, to answer Ellee's question, creating a 'Wisdom' educational program for children, including the etheric structure, mental, astral, and physical-etheric forms, would primarily be a responsibility of a portion of the 'teaching' petal or 'Teaching Group' of the Group Heart Center.

"Moving that educational program outward, subjectively and objectively, would be a responsibility of the aura of that teaching petal.

"This creative activity would be part of the activity, function, and unfolding purpose of the teaching petal,

Heart Center, and Group Unit, and would be supported by the functions of the other petals, centers, and Ashramic Units in various ways, with some providing more active, immediate support than others.

"However, all of this begins and is supported by recognition of function. The disciple —Unit, Center, or petal— take up their work when they recognize their function, and their coworkers support those efforts by also recognizing that function.

"That recognition of function is achieved via persistent, focused, performance of the inner work."

Arista: "Let's see if I have this. The pre-existing position of our Overshadowing Spiritual Soul predicates our spiritual work, and predisposes us to certain energies, talents, tasks, and forms of service."

Quinn: "Partly, yes, but it needs clarifying.

"There are seven basic types of consciousness — which types are normally described by us a ray 'energies', but those rays are also types of consciousness.

"Each type of consciousness is part of a vast consciousness of the Ashram of that Ray.

"Each Ray Ashram has, in potential, seven subsidiary ashrams, each of which has its own group of ashramic consciousness.

"Within the ashramic consciousness are groups of consciousness, consisting of individualized Spiritual Souls, which share a relationship with a portion of the purpose of the Ashram, and thus a common function within the group life of the Ashram.

"In the Sixth Ray age the goal —the path of return— of aspirational spiritual disciples was, in effect, to move up into and at-one with the Overshadowing Spiritual Soul —to attain and remain in the group life of the Soul in the Ashram.

"In the Seventh Ray age the goal is to at-one with

the Ashramic Group, precipitate that Group Life into the three lower worlds, and reflect that precipitated life into the world of affairs.

"That is what the inner work, the Magic of Consciousness, is about. It is a method whereby we unify our inner spiritual life and our outer life and affairs.

"Thus, who we are as Spiritual Soul determines our function within our Group, of our Group within the Ashram, and of the Ashram within the Planetary Life.

"The Soul builds characteristics into the persona instrument that will predispose it towards and enable it to take the next step in the process.

"Thus, one can discover one's place and function within the greater life by both ascending to union with that life, and looking around to see where you are within it, and by looking at the patterns of thought, feeling, and activity built into your instrument to see what type of work it has been built to perform.

"In any case, in this age that place will be an Ashramic Group Unit, and that function will be an expression of Group Discipleship.

"Now, it's about that time, are there any questions before closing? OK, we'll close in the usual fashion.

Closing Meditation

Quinn: "As a group, renew the upward line of indigo-white light from the group ajna, through the group crown center, to the Wisdom and that portion of the Wisdom overshadowing the group. (pause)

"As a group in the ajna, invoke that portion of the Wisdom, including that related to the Ashram of Synthesis, downward, through the three lower worlds and into the group brain awareness, by audibly sounding the OM. (long pause)

"From the ajna, project that Wisdom outward into appearance in the group life and affairs by again audibly sounding the OM. (long pause)

"From the ajna, align the group brain upward, via a line of indigo-white light, back up to the overshadowing Wisdom. Again, audibly sound the OM. (pause)

"Leaving the alignment in place, slowly relax the attention and return to this here and now.

Chapter 3

Postscript

As soon as we pulled out of the alley onto the street, he asked, "What did you see?"

"Their aura was... less resistant, more..."

"Permeable"

"Yes. It allowed more in, didn't resist as much, and when it did, well, it wasn't as bad."

"They're doing quite well, really. In some ways it's a good first experience for you, to see what can be done with a group like this. With most you have to take it much slower and easier. Years instead of weeks. If you hit a group with to much too quick, they'll shatter as the polarities erupt."

"How do you know how much?"

"You don't, and... well, it's not our job to keep them together, to determine how much. They do that, they determine *how much* via their invocative strength, and whether they'll *stay together* via their focus on their purpose."

"We're not responsible?"

I watched the lights in the center of his head flicker while we waited for a traffic signal. The signal turned green, and as we moved forward, he said, "We're responsible for *our* function. Look, always, always remember this. A very large part of what we do is to enable people to *be responsible*, to be able to respond, to *act as Soul*. We can't do that if we take responsibility *for* them, and if we do, well... there will always be those groups that invoke more than they can handle, and break up. If they won't take responsibility, but we do, then they'll blame us and we'll accept it. That's not a place you want to be."

His voice trailed into a quivering E-flat, and dark yellow stirred throughout his aura. He'd been there, accepted blame for such a break, and the imprint of the pain still tormented him.

Chapter 4

The Ashram of Synthesis

Zed's smile crinkled the corners of his eyes, and the group aura radiated blue and vibrated with a clear E-sharp drone. Myron was back in his place, and the auras of both he and Hal were quiet and clear. Amanda embraced me, and then so did the rest of the women, one by one.

Quinn found his seat and began composing the alignment as I set up our things. He completed the indigo-white cone, the room grew still, and I turned on the recorder.

Opening Alignment

"Move into the ajna and integrate the three-fold persona into a single unit.

"From the ajna, align upward via a line of indigo-white through the crown center to and with that portion of the Wisdom which overshadows Group Discipleship.

"From the ajna, invoke that portion of the Wisdom related to Group Discipleship downward into appearance by audibly sounding the OM. (long pause)

"From the ajna, project that Wisdom outward to the group brain awareness by again audibly sounding the OM.

"From the ajna, align the group brain upward, via a line of indigo-white light, directly to the overshadowing Wisdom. Again, audibly sound the OM. (pause)

"Leaving this triangular alignment in place, slowly relax the attention and return to your normal focus."

Chapter 4

The Ashram of Synthesis

Quinn: "Well, we've been through the basics on the new Magic, Organization, and Discipleship. The portion of the Wisdom overshadowing us this evening includes everything the disciple needs to know about this new Ashram in order to take up our Disciplic place and function in right relationship with that Ashram. So, our aim this evening is to precipitate as much of that Wisdom, as much understanding of the purpose, place, and function of the Ashram, as we can.

"Now, it appears that after considerable preparation, on or around Wesak of 1946 Masters M., D.K., and R. formulated a new Ashram, with part of the 'personnel' — if one can use that term— from their Ashrams and with themselves as a threefold monad at the heart of the new Ashram. Depending on one's perspective, this new Ashram is variously known as 'The Ashram of Synthesis', 'The Synthetic Ashram', and 'The Synthesis Ashram'.

"Yes Zed?"

Zed: "That's the Ashram described in the Wesak Message of 1946?" [21]

Quinn: "Yes."

"The primary purpose of this Ashram is to help prepare humanity to take initiation, as a kingdom, at the end of this age. As part of this process, it is partly responsible for shifting civilization from a Sixth Ray to a Seventh Ray impulse, and for shifting the method of organizing substance from a Third Ray structure to a Seventh. It is of course aided in these tasks by the other ashrams —which it aids in turn— but the new Ashram bears the primary responsibility for this particular task.[22]

---

[21] *The Externalization of the Hierarchy*, by Alice A. Bailey, p. 541

[22] *Ashramic Projections*, by Lucille Cedercrans, pp. 35-37, 41, 47-49

"Nyle?"

Nyle: "Why wait until 1946 to create this ashram?"

Quinn: "The Hierarchy? Well, actually, they didn't. You see, a, not the same exactly, but an equivalent ashram existed in Atlantean times, with much the same task then as now. But, well, you all know what happened. We failed and Atlantis fell."

Me: "We?"

(A wisp of yellowish-brown appeared in Quinn's aura near his abdomen, but quickly dissipated.)

Quinn: "Yes. The 'new' Ashram includes many of the 'personnel' of the old. Our work was so entwined with what happened then, that the fall of Atlantis shattered the Ashram. Its souls were scattered, thrown back into the animal man stage, and spent many ages coming back, walking the path anew —if more quickly since we'd been over it before. And now, finally, we're reaching the point where we can take up the work again, and find redemption for our past failure.

(The group quieted, a bit uncomfortable, radiating a hint of the pale-violet light of compassion.)

"Now, given this task, the new Ashram is also responsible, to an extent, for the transition from the old 'individual' method of initiation, through group initiation, to initiation of the entire human kingdom.[23] Thus, from this perspective, 'group initiation' is a transitional —if crucial— process. Within this new Ashram:

"The Master M. holds the Positive Pole of Divine Purpose,

"The Master D.K. holds the Magnetic Field of Divine Relationship,

"and, in this context, the Master R. holds the 'Negative' Pole of Ceremonial Magic or of manifestation.

---

[23] *Ashramic Projections*, by Lucille Cedercrans, pp. 117-120

Chapter 4

The Ashramic Group Life

"The monads at the heart of the Ashram are of course surrounded by the Consciousness of the Ashram, which is held in relationship by the Substance of the Ashram. Now, I don't recall how Bailey puts this, but as you may be aware the sheath or individualizing light body of the Spiritual Soul of the initiate is shattered at the fourth initiation. As a result, a master does not have an individualized Spiritual Soul. Thus, the Soul of the Master is the Soul of the Ashram; or, from our perspective, all of the Souls of the Ashram are, collectively, the Soul of the Master. Also, the instruments of those Souls —buddhic light bodies, mental, astral, physical-etheric and physical-dense— are, collectively, the body of the Master.

"Thus, from this perspective, a Master is fully in incarnation only when every portion of his Ashramic Group Life has precipitated itself into the three lower worlds, as a functioning unit of Ashramic Group Consciousness.

"Now, as we've already discussed Group Discipleship, it should not be surprising that this Ashramic Life consists of Group Units or Disciples each of which has a place and function within the Ashram, and each of which is, in a sense, the equivalent of a chakra in the instrument of the Monad.

"Each Group Unit is a formulation of the three aspects of the Ashram —of purpose, consciousness, precipitation."

Hal: "Of all three Rays?"

Quinn: "Ummm... I'd rather not describe it in terms of rays. In this context, the three monads are three aspects of the Ashram, unified into a single point. As a result, each aspect is distributed equally, throughout the Ashramic Life and within each Group Unit. Thus, each Unit includes all three aspects as a united whole rather than just as distinct parts.

"Within each Group Unit those three aspects are further formulated into Group Centers —a group Crown Center, Synthetic or Cave Center, Ajna Center, Throat Center, and Heart Center. Now, entire courses could be taught on any one of these Group Centers. However, very basically:

"The Group Crown or Head Center is responsible for holding the focus on the Purpose of the Group.

"The Group Cave or Synthesis Center is responsible for formulating and holding the group purpose, relationship, and intelligent activity into a synthetic whole.

"The Group Ajna Center is responsible for precipitating the synthetic whole via the group persona, and for aligning the embodied group with the overshadowing.

"The Group Throat Center is responsible for the intelligent activity which manifests the group work and life.

"The Group Heart Center is responsible for holding the group in right relationship —within itself and with the greater life of which it is a part— in part via the flow of the life of the group.

"Hal?"

Hal: "So that's First Ray Head Center, Second Ajna, Third Throat, Fourth Heart, and what, Synthetic Cave?"

Quinn: "Oh, not quite. You see, that's *structure*, and we're more concerned here with *function*. For instance, the Group Throat Center works more with the Seventh Ray energy of Organization and the Ajna with Second, but in this case those are, well, sub-tones of the Energy of Synthesis, while the Group Cave works directly with

Chapter 4

Synthesis Energy.

"Each group center has, in potential, both esoteric — subjective— and exoteric —objective— expressions. Also, each group center also has a similar basic structure, which consists of a formulation of the three aspects of that center —a Center Nucleus, Center Petals, and Center Aura.

> "The Center Nucleus is responsible for holding the alignment upward with the purpose at the heart of the Group Unit, and through that Unit with the Purpose of the Ashram.

> "The various Center Petals are responsible for formulating a portion of the center function into a particular service activity —a heart center might have a petal responsible for healing and another responsible for teaching, etc.

> "The aura of each petal —a portion of the aura of the center— is responsible for holding the outward alignment, radiating the will, quality, and character of the petal out to the body receptive of that petal. The personnel of the aura consists of those who have been called to that center, but not to any specific function in that center.

"The personnel of the center nucleus and petals will consist of those called to that particular function within that center, within that Ashramic Group Unit. Those functions are exclusive in the sense that one can perform only one such function at a time and for a worker to move from one function to another is a significant change.

"All of these functions are interrelated in an organic sense. That is, none exist, none can exist apart from the others —any more than a finger exists apart from its hand."

Hugh: "The Wisdom Group is one of these Group Units?"

Quinn: "Yes. The Group Unit known as 'The Wisdom Group' is responsible for making the Wisdom available to humanity.

(Several people tried to speak at once.)

"Hold on, let me continue a bit.

"Now, as I've mentioned before, my function within the Wisdom Group is within the Group Heart Center, as part of the Nucleus of that Center, so naturally I am most familiar with that Group Unit and that Center within the Group.

"Like any center, the Wisdom Group Heart Center has a number of petals —in various stages of manifestation. Each of those Heart Center petals has a function within that of the Heart Center, including petals responsible for healing, teaching, etc."

Angelique: "Is that related to the 'Teaching Group'?"

Quinn: "The 'teaching petal' is another way of describing it, yes.

"For those of you who don't know, some of Lucille's material indicates that a 'Teacher of the Wisdom' is part of a 'Teaching Group'. From our current perspective, the 'Teaching Group' is the teaching petal of the Wisdom Group Heart Center.

"Now, the creative activity of the Teaching Group would involve the magical process whereby the Wisdom is moved out to those who need it —in whatever manner, level, and form they are ready to receive it— and then relate them back up directly to the Wisdom, and through the Wisdom to their own place and function within the One Life.

"In this context, creating, for instance, a 'Wisdom' educational program for children —including the etheric structure, mental, astral, and physical-etheric forms— would primarily be a responsibility of a portion of the teaching petal of the Group Heart Center.

100

Chapter 4

"This creative activity would be part of the activity, function, and unfolding purpose of the teaching petal, Heart Center, and Group Unit, and would be supported by the functions of the other petals, centers, and Ashramic Units in various ways, with some providing more active, immediate support than others.

"For instance, while moving that education program outward, subjectively and objectively, would be a responsibility of the aura of that teaching petal, organizing that outward movement would be part of the responsibility of the Group Throat Center. In a sense, the aura is the movement, and the Throat Center organizes that movement, along Seventh Ray lines of course.

"All the Group Units and the entire Ashram functions in this way, with each portion supporting the others by performing their function. However, it all begins with the recognition of function. The disciple —Unit, Center, or petal— take up their work as and when they recognize their function, and their coworkers support those efforts by also recognizing that function.

"That recognition of function is achieved via persistent, focused, performance of the inner work."

Arista: "What exactly is this 'Wisdom' you keep referring to. I'd assumed it was a reinterpretation of the Ageless Wisdom, but you talk about it as though it's something else."

The New Thought-Form Presentation of the Wisdom

"Well, it depends on how you approach it. For instance, the Ageless Wisdom is sometimes defined as that unchanging Truth which has always been available to humanity, in some form, in every time and place. However, from a more Seventh Ray perspective, the Ageless

101

Wisdom is the Divine Plan, precipitated by the Hierarchy into buddhic substance where it becomes the Idea of
Truth, and into mental substance where it becomes the
thought-form of Truth.

"Now, from our current perspective 'the Wisdom' is
distinct to the purpose and function of the Synthesis
Ashram.

"In the process of creating the new Ashram, M.,
D.K., and R. held the Spiritual Purpose of the Ashram
—a portion of the Divine Plan— in a tight focus, and
projected that purpose downward in frequency into the
buddhic plane. Sounding its note within the buddhic,
the Ashramic Plan attracted resonant buddhic substance into a new Idea of Truth.

"This Idea is known in Lucille's materials as 'The
New Thought-form Presentation of the Wisdom', the
'NTFPW', or 'the Wisdom'.

"Portions of this Idea are in turn projected downward and held focused within the upper mental plane,
where it attracts resonant mental substance. That mental substance then formulates the precipitated Idea into
a 'thought-form', which is also known as 'the Wisdom'.

"So, when you look at what they are and how they
are created, you can say that 'the Wisdom', being a precipitation of a part of the Plan, is in a sense a part of the
Ageless Wisdom, and, you can say that the Wisdom,
being a precipitation of the purpose of the new Ashram,
is a distinct thing in itself. Both views are correct. It
just depends on how you look at it.

"Now, it's important to keep our role in mind while
looking at this process. The Masters at the heart of the
Ashram were able to do this because the incarnate portions of the Ashramic Group Life, the Disciplic Units of
the ashram, were functioning as the invocative negative
pole —up to that point.

102

Chapter 4

"However, from that point it becomes the task of those Disciplic Group Units to relate that Idea and that Thought-form to a similarly invocative body-receptive within humanity. In other words, it is the particular task of the Wisdom Group to continue precipitating the Idea into the three lower worlds, and the task of the students of the Wisdom to invoke the Wisdom into appearance! Thus, the process requires the coordinated efforts of the masters, the Group Units, and the body receptive. Otherwise, the Wisdom would remain overshadowing, unprojected, and unmanifest, a mere mental abstraction.

"It is during the precipitation into the concrete mental that the thought-form takes on a form, such as words, music, etc., that the persona can identify. However, that form remains subjective until the precipitation process is complete, and the Wisdom is given appearance as spoken or written words, audible music, etc.

"Arista?"

Arista: "So 'the Wisdom' is precipitated via the Magic of Consciousness?"

Quinn: "Yes. And the body receptive to the Wisdom is aligned back up, directly with the Wisdom, via the same magical process.

"Now, the incarnate consciousness is attracted to the written material because of a relationship with the Ashramic Purpose embodied in that material. It's the frequency of motivating purpose within and behind it that attracts the consciousness, usually because that consciousness, on Soul Levels, is already identified with and resonating to that purpose.

"In other words, the Soul on its plane is already a part of the Ashram, has its life and affairs within that Ashram, and thus the teachings sound and feel like 'home'.

"If the Soul is not part of the Synthesis Ashram, then it will be within another Ashram and will be working with this material temporarily as part of its next step.

"In any case, that Soul will be working to precipitate its Soul Life, its place and function within its Group Unit, into the three lower worlds. The Soul will be precipitating its function as a coordinated part of the Group function, and the Group will be precipitating itself as part of the Ashramic function.

"Thus, as students come together in consciousness and demand the appearance of the Wisdom via coordinated invocative work, they are moving toward the realization of their purpose, place, and function within the Ashram.

"Now, there are several points to keep in mind in this. One is that the Ashram of Synthesis, and the NTFPW, were and are being formulated using the very magical process which is a part of the teachings.

"The teachings are an expression of the Ashram, a partial precipitation of the NTFPW. There are and will be other such precipitations."

Celine: "Groups, teachings, what?"

Quinn: "Well, the materials indicate that Lucille was one of seven 'Disciples on the Thread' from the Synthesis Ashram who incarnated at approximately the same time —following some incarnations of preparation— for the express purpose of bringing The New Thought-form Presentation of the Wisdom to humanity.[24] Each of these Disciples had their own particular purpose within the greater purpose of the Ashram, expressed that purpose in their own way, and that did not always include teaching classes or writing.

"There are at least seven Group Units within the Ashram, each expressing its portion of the Ashramic Purpose in its own way."

------

[24] Glen: This is mentioned in *Applied Wisdom*, by Lucille Cedercrans, which is scheduled for publication in 2005

104

Chapter 4

"Myron?"

Myron: "Are each of these Units on their own subray, like subsidiary ashrams?"

Quinn: "Ummm. Let's be careful here. Remember, this is the Synthesis Ashram —it's not organized quite the same way as the others, it's still forming, and some of the Units aren't clear enough to 'see' yet. Not for me, anyway.

"Remember, most of the major ashrams described by D.K. were not yet complete even then. This is also true of the Synthesis Ashram. But more and more workers, individuals and Group Units, are taking up their task, and thus the Wisdom is increasingly being precipitated into the mental, astral, physical-etheric, and reflected into the physical-dense.

"Depending on where a group and individual are focused, they can pick it up and reinterpret it at any of these levels, and on up to the buddhic Idea and the monadic Intent. Lucille's printed materials provide a physical-dense key upward, to whatever level of contact one is able to reach. But, if one has a clear and steady alignment, one may connect with the astral force, mental energy, or buddhic Idea of the Wisdom without those or any other texts.

"Hal?"

Hal: "So why's it called 'the Wisdom Group'. When I first heard *that* it sounded, so, well arrogant, self important."

Quinn: (Grinning.) "Well, arrogance is one of the glamours many of us have to deal with. It's a natural consequence of that sense of self-importance that comes with having something others don't. But that passes as one embodies the teachings, as one *becomes* Wisdom.

"As for why 'the Wisdom Group', remember what 'the Wisdom' is in this context. It's a contraction of 'The New Thought-form Presentation of the Wisdom', that Idea of Truth which includes everything humanity needs and must have to take initiation, as a kingdom, at the end of this age. The Wisdom Group is that Ashramic Group Unit which has the primary responsibility of conveying that Idea to humanity. That is our motivating Group Purpose, our Life.

"Now, when that Group Purpose was sounded within the Ashram, it attracted both the resonant substance and resonant consciousness of the Ashram. So, the Wisdom is that portion of the Soul Light of the Ashram which formulated that Purpose into an Idea, and the Wisdom Group is that portion of the Ashramic Consciousness which identified with that Purpose.

"So, you have the Purpose, Consciousness, and Substance of the Group Unit. The New Thought-form Presentation of the Wisdom is, in a sense, the Substance of the Ashram which is in our care, for which we are particularly responsible. So, you could say it's 'The New Thought-form Presentation of the Wisdom Group', and that's just been shortened to 'The Wisdom Group'.

"Ellee?"

Ellee: "I've been studying the Ageless Wisdom for decades, but I didn't hear about Lucille's stuff until a few years ago. If this 'Wisdom' is so important, why isn't it out there? Why don't you hear more about it?"

Quinn: "Well, there are a number of reasons for that. Up until 1995 the emphasis of the work was intentionally and necessarily on the more Seventh Ray work of precipitating the Ashram into appearance. This was the emphasis for the first forty-nine years, seven cycles of seven cycles. It had to be, because the basic structure for moving the teaching out, for precipitating the Energy of Synthesis, did not exist."

Myron: "You had to build the structure, to organize the Ashram first?"

Chapter 4

Devas of Synthesis

Quinn: "No... Well, yes, but as part of that building work we had to attract substance that resonated with the Ashramic Purpose, and impress it with that Purpose. We had to build a new order of Devas of Synthesis.

"This new order of devas is created as the Ashramic Group Units work the magical process. There are a number of points overshadowing this, and I will attempt to outline some of them.

"First, regarding the new order of Devas of Synthesis, what they are, why they are necessary, and how they come into being.

"Some of this is answered, in part, by a definition of the new order: The Devas of Synthesis are those devas —of whatever frequency, Buddhic, mental energy, astral force, or etheric substance— who are created via the ceremonial activity of Synthesis and act as a medium of the Energy of Synthesis.

"A prime example of this type of deva is the etheric network that holds together and which constitutes the soul body of the Ashram of Synthesis. That etheric network is a body of Buddhic Light, the Soul Light of the Ashram, which enfolds and interconnects the Group Units within the Ashramic Group Life, and serves as a telepathic medium between those Units, the Monad of Synthesis at the heart of the Ashram, and each other. It's all one Synthetic deva, the Buddhic body or instrument of the Ashram, but it's composed of many devas, such as the deva of each Unit.

"So, each Group Unit or Disciple within the Ashram is a portion of the consciousness of the Ashram, and has its associated portion of the instrument of the Ashram. In effect, the Buddhic light body of a Group Unit is a subtle organ or chakra within the Buddhic Instrument of the Ashram.

"Thus, as a Group Unit performs its task, projecting its Ashramic function into the three lower worlds and reflecting itself therein, it creates a reflection of its portion of the Ashramic Instrument in mental energy, astral force, and physical-etheric substance. Each of these reflections is a deva, a deva of Synthesis formulated on that level and carrying, on that level and via that Unit, the quality and synthesizing effect of the Energy of Synthesis.

"As each Unit continues to perform its work, it naturally formulates a growing constellation of Devas of Synthesis to carry out various portions of that work. The result is a growing host of angelic beings, each with their particular characteristics and functions, but all created via and instruments of Synthesis.

"You will note that the type of work that creates these devas is carried out by Ashramic Group Units, not by individuals. Individuals are involved in this creative process as part of Group Units, but it is the nature of that sort of work that one does not perform it 'alone', but only as part of, in close identification with and within, a Group Unit.

"Since these devas are created by the magical work of Group Units of the Synthesis Ashram, they naturally respond to the intent of the Ashram as conveyed to them by its Group Units. Their function is to formulate the Ashramic Purpose into those synthetic mental, astral, and physical-etheric forms which will embody the ashramic purpose and function. They are the organized Intelligent Activity of the Ashram.

"Now, because their function includes embodying and conveying the Wisdom to humanity, the Wisdom could not be conveyed to humanity until those devas were in place.

"Yes, Ellee?"

Chapter 4

Ellee: "Why not? Why couldn't they just, well, pick up a book and read it?"

Quinn: "Well, any such book would, of necessity, be an embodiment of the Wisdom in the three lower worlds, a reflection in time and space. The Devas of Synthesis are that 'embodiment', the substance in which the Wisdom is formulated and which is in turn reflected as a book, or whatever, in time and space. So, without the devas it can't be embodied.

"And then there's the question of, well, how did that person happen to 'find' that book at the time when they were ready for it? How were they able to 'connect' with that book physically, emotionally, mentally, and spiritually? The Devas of Synthesis *are* those actual, substantial connections! With them in place, the outer connection is inevitable; it appears to just arrange itself. Without them, it can't happen.

"Now, because of this, those consciously working in the Ashram of Synthesis knew from the beginning that it would be a long time —in persona terms— before the Ashram and its work gained the recognition and cooperation of coworkers in and/or identified with other Ashrams. Most of those who entered the Ashram's work in the 1950s grew old and died without every seeing any recognition, and without knowing if their lifetime's work would bear any outer fruit.

"This is why members of that group life appear defensive at times. Acceptance by trained occultists has been very rare —practically nonexistent— until quite recently. We simply are not accustomed to it.

"Zed?"

Zed: "We'd never do that!"

Quinn: "You've always been very polite, yes, but when did the center begin selling copies of *The Nature of the Soul* and allowing the class to be taught here?"

Zed: "Uh... 1997, '98."

Quinn: "Yes. With the completion of the forty-nine year building period in 1995, the emphasis of the work shifted from training workers and building the ashramic mechanism to educating humanity.[25] In a sense, this can be seen as a transfer in the primary activity of the Ashram from Seventh Ray to Second —while the overshadowing ashramic energy remains that of Synthesis.

"One effect of this change in emphasis is that the Ashram and its work is becoming more visible to and easily recognized by those identified with Second Ray teachings. Before that it was almost invisible, and when occultists encountered it they tended to see what they expected to see, something familiar rather than what it is.

"For average humanity, this change will mean an increasing appearance of the Wisdom in their daily life and affairs, without any particular conscious brain awareness of what it is or where it came from. It will just be something that they're drawn to, that makes sense, and that works."

Arista: "If I understand what you're saying, the various grades of Synthesis Devas are created as the Group Units precipitate the Ashramic Purpose downward into substance. Those devas then become the instrument of what, the Plan of Synthesis? A synthesis of what? What's that Plan?"

———————————————

[25] Glen: One of the first expressions of this shift was *Ashramic Projections*, by Lucille Cedercrans, a series of booklets published by Wisdom Impressions in 1997. This series included information on the creative process, Synthesis Ashram, Ashramic Group Life, and Group Initiation that had not previously been publicly available. The *Ashramic Projections* series was expanded and published as a book in 2004.

Chapter 4

The Energy of Synthesis

Quinn: "Oh, my. Well, I'll take the easier part first and explain Synthesis, and then go to the 'Plan of Synthesis'.

"Usually I would define 'synthesis' as the lifting in frequency of any subsidiary seven into its original, over-shadowing source. For instance, the Seven Planetary Rays will eventually be 'synthesized' into the Third Solar Ray, and the Seven Solar Rays will be 'synthesized' into the Second Cosmic Ray. Thus, the Second Cosmic Ray is the Synthetic Ray of the Solar System.

So, 'synthesis' is a process of reunion, and what 'synthesis energy' is depends on what one is reuniting. For instance, you will recall that I earlier defined the terms 'Synthetic Ashram', 'Ashram of Synthesis', and 'Synthesis Ashram' as referring to the same Ashram, but via different approaches. The 'Energy of Synthesis' is directly related to this.

"The synthesis of portions of the First, a Second, and the Seventh Ray ashrams into a new 'Synthetic Ashram' produced or included a synthesis of the Rays of those ashrams. This new Synthetic Energy, a synthesis of First, Second, and Seventh, is the Synthetic Energy which one experiences and wields as one ascends to and becomes at-one within the Synthetic Ashram.

"So, from this perspective, 'Synthetic Energy' is a synthesis of First, Second, and Seventh that one experiences and utilizes while ascending through the aura and periphery of the Synthetic Ashram.

"As one moves into the Ashram as part of a working Group Unit, and takes up one's place and function therein, one participates in the ashramic function of receiving Energy from the Higher Triangle, stepping that Energy down in frequency, and radiating it outward as the Energy of Synthesis.

"As the group moves into its place in the Ashramic Group Life and takes up its function, it utilizes the 'Energy of Synthesis' as part of its work. Precisely what that work is will, of course, vary considerably from group to group —which is why Lucille's works discuss group work in general, except on those occasions when it is directed to a particular group and function.

"Let's see... There was something..."

Me: "'The Plan of Synthesis'."

Synthesis

Monad

Quinn: "Oh, right, the more difficult point. Umm...

"Now, there are a variety of ways of looking at the Synthesis Ashram, and how one does so and what one perceives is affected in large part by one's perspective, that is, one's position —in the world of affairs, in the three lower worlds, or within the Ashram— and one's consciousness —Ray, etc.

"Within the Ashram, the attention of the Ashramic Group Units or Group Disciples is primarily directed at the point of monadic purpose at the heart of the Ashram. That point of purpose, the Seed of Life of the Ashram, is not experienced by those Units as 'a synthesis of M., D.K., and R'. It is experienced by those Units as '*a*' life, as *a* Synthetic Monad or Monad of Synthesis — depending, again, on whether one is aspiring to or precipitating.

"One can picture this by imagining what happens when one holds three stones in a horizontal equilateral triangle over a pool of water, and drops them simultaneously. The stones fall, strike the water at the same time, and each stone creates a series of rings or waves moving out from the point of impact, and intersecting each other as they radiate outward. At the points where any two waves meet they combine for a moment, forming a larger crest before moving on. However, in the center of the triangle, all three waves meet simultaneously, and form a mound that is the sum of the three. This mound collapses, and in turn forms its own waves which move out from the center.

"Now, imagine that instead of stones the waves are formed by three radiating points of purpose. The outward moving waves are constant, and thus so is the point at the center. That point of purpose is a synthesis of the three, with its own tone, quality, and life.

"In this case, that central point is the Synthetic Monad at the heart of the Ashram of Synthesis.

"Now consider this —we have already discussed the concept of the New Path of Group Initiation, of Group Discipleship, a path which none of the Masters in the Hierarchy have experienced, but which is the current path of initiation. However, at the heart of the Synthesis Ashram, which bears the primary responsibility for formulating this new path, is a *Synthetic Monad* formed via a higher correspondent of that new path.

"So, the 'Master' to which the Group Units aspire, to which they direct their attention, and from which they receive their purpose, is not M., D.K., or R., or a combination of them, but the Monad of Synthesis."

Celine: "Who brings through this 'Energy of Synthesis'."

Quinn: "Yes."

Nyle: "From the Avatar of Synthesis?"

Quinn: "From a Higher Triangle that includes the Avatar."

Nyle: "He's an avatar of Cosmic First, so the Synthetic Energy would be Cosmic First Ray."

Energy

Quinn: "Well, no. That's what he brought, but it's not what we receive. You see... well, consider the Law of Correspondences, 'as above so below'. Just as the synthetic center in the head, the cave, and each Group Unit, and the Monad of Synthesis, are formed via the at-one-ment of the Three Aspects at that level, so is the Higher Triangle that overshadows the Synthesis Ashram.

"That Higher Triangle consists of the Avatar of Synthesis, the Christ, and the Planetary Logos. In this Triangle the Avatar holds the First Ray point, the Christ the Second, the Logos the Third, and together they formulate a point of synthesis.

"Nyle?"

Nyle: "In *Externalization* the Tibetan indicates that the Avatar of Synthesis is pouring his energy into a triangle formed of The Christ, the Master Morya, and the Manu."[26]

Quinn: (Smiling softly, and speaking in friendly tones.) "That was one of Alice's later works, published, what, in the mid 50s? Have you looked lately?

"The planetary life continues to grow and develop, and these things change. As part of our work, the Ashramic Group Unit of which I am a part has reached through the Monad and... touched... the Higher Triangle. What we found was a Triangle of The Avatar of Synthesis, the Christ, and the Planetary Logos. The Avatar was part of this invocative triangle, and what was being received by that triangle was, well, I really can't describe it but 'Cosmic Second' is perhaps close.

"The Planetary Life appears to be building a series

---

[26] Quinn: *The Externalization of the Hierarchy,* by Alice A. Bailey, p. 663

of triangles, composed of the Three Aspects, which together focus and create a synthetic or 'cave' center at the heart of each triangle. This triangular structure is being constructed all the way from the highest point of the planetary life down to its lowest, and it appears to be intimately related to the Purpose of the Planetary Life within the Cosmic Life.

"Thus, this Higher Triangle of:

"The Avatar of Synthesis —as a First Ray point,

"The Overshadowing Christ —as a Second Ray point— and,

"The Planetary Logos —as a Third Ray point—

"have formulated a Synthetic or Cave Center which invokes, focuses, and radiates 'Cosmic Second'.

"In this context, the Cosmic First brought by the Avatar provided the motivation that initiated the process.

"This same basic triangular formation is used to build and access the cave or synthetic center at every 'level' —if we can use that term in this regard— and it is via the Cave at each level of its expression that the Energy of Synthesis is invoked, focused, and radiated.

"Now, the 'Cosmic Second Ray' invoked by this Higher Triangle is stepped down in frequency by that Triangle, and radiated down and outward.

"That Synthesis is then received by the Monad of Synthesis at the heart of the Ashram of Synthesis, stepped down in frequency again, and precipitated into the life, consciousness, and activity of the Ashram.

"The Ashramic Group Life receives that Synthesis Energy, radiates it outward —making it available to Group Units or disciples in other ashrams— and steps it downward —precipitating it toward humanity.

"Those ideas are in turn precipitated into the mental

plane by the Group Units, where the Synthetic Devas of the mental plane give them shape and form as the New Thought-form Presentation of the Wisdom.

"So, what is being developed, then, is a series of triangular centers for receiving, transforming, and broadcasting the purpose, consciousness, and substance of Synthesis.

"Now, having said all that, we can finally get to the why, 'the Plan of Synthesis'.

Purpose

"The answer is in the nature of the consciousness and devic substance involved. From the perspective of the Magic of Consciousness, it is the function of consciousness to relate Purpose or Intent to Substance, and to relate the Intelligent Activity of Substance to Purpose, in a mutually causal interaction of those poles that brings about their re-union. Thus, it is the function of the consciousness or magnetic field of the Synthesis Ashram to relate the purpose of that Ashram to the substance which is negative or receptive to that purpose.

"However, at this point the Ashram encountered one of its first tasks or challenges. There were no devas in this system that were capable of receiving, responding to, and carrying the Energy of Synthesis. Thus, one of the initial tasks of the consciousness of the Ashram was to 'formulate' the new order of 'Devas of Synthesis', creating intelligent substance that is particularly sensitive and responsive to the Energy of Synthesis.

"Formulating this new order of devas was absolutely crucial, for while the consciousness relates the two poles via awareness, the deva carries out or embodies that awareness. Thus, the quality of consciousness and the frequency of energy which is the Energy of Synthesis could not be expressed until and unless there were

116

devas who were capable of doing so.

"As I mentioned, this work of formulating an order of Devas of Synthesis is proceeding, and partly due to progress in that direction it is now vastly easier to be conscious of and to express synthesis in the three lower worlds than it was in the middle of the last century. And it is at this point that the Purpose of Synthesis becomes apparent.

"As some of you will recall, the 'formulae' of the Divine Plan is described in Lesson One of The Nature of the Soul, on page...

(Quinn turned, walked over to a sales table, plucked a copy of N.S. from a display, and began flipping pages).

"Ah, top of page nineteen, second through fourth lines:

"'The combination or synthesis of Purpose, Evolution, and Activity which will finally manifest as The Christ in outer expression, we refer to as the Divine Plan.'

(Quinn returned the book to the table, strode over to the dry-erase board, and picked up a pen.)

"Now, what does that mean, 'synthesis of Purpose, Evolution, and Activity'?

"If we look at it from a more Fifth Ray perspective — if my faint recollections of college math is correct— we get something like this:

(Quinn drew the following equation on the board, put the pen down, and returned to his seat.)

"$((P + E + A) = C) = DP$

"So, that Synthesis of the Three Aspects, which equals the Christ, equals the Divine Plan. Or, to turn it around, The Divine Plan is 'to manifest the Christ on Earth by Synthesizing the Three Aspects of Divinity'.

"This will, of course, be accomplished slowly, over many ages. As the Purpose, Consciousness, and Devas of Synthesis unite in the planetary life, Earth will become a radiant Center of Synthesis within the Solar Life. At that point, it will be Earth's particular karmic responsibility to radiate the Purpose, Consciousness, and Substance of Synthesis into the Solar Life. That work will include an expansion of the Consciousness of Synthesis and the Intelligent Activity of Synthesis from the Planetary into the Solar Life.

"Of course, the Law of Correspondences suggests that the work now being done on Earth within the Ashram of Synthesis will be the same work that is done, on a larger scale, by the planetary life within the Solar Life. However, the work of Synthesis does not end there.

"The Earth is in effect a laboratory for synthesizing opposites, which gives this planetary and solar system a peculiar significance in the Universal Life.

"Have any of you heard of 'seed crystals'? Well, apparently when a substance begins to form into a crystalline shape, such as ice freezing into water, it begins at a point where the first crystal forms, and then the crystal spreads throughout its medium. And when creating a crystal, one can insert a tiny seed crystal into the medium, and the medium then crystallizes around that, following its pattern.

"Well, Earth is, or will be, a sort of seed crystal in the Universe. Not the only one, perhaps, but a crucial one.

"Now, remember what I've said about the Cave or Synthesis Center? It's formed via or at the center of the union of the Three Aspects —the First, Second, and Third— and because that union is created by Consciousness rather than Substance it's not differentiated into many but remains one. There's only *one* Cave, *one* Synthesis Center.

"So, the Earth is developing into a Center of Cosmic Synthesis, a Cave Center within the Solar Life. And we all know that at some point after the Reappearance the

118

Chapter 4

Christ, the 'Lord Maitreya' will move on and K.H. will take up that office. However, at some point in the distant future Maitreya will return to Earth as the Cosmic Christ.

"But why? Why return to Earth? Well, what happens when the Cosmic Christ moves into a Center of Synthesis? That center, that quality and activity of synthesis, is related to every receptive consciousness and deva in the entire Universe.

"The result can only be synthesis on a cosmic scale, not a 'bang-whimper', but a 'bang-synthesis'.[27]

"So, that's our purpose. Humanity is the planetary brain, currently functioning as the throat center, but we will eventually —via the Magic of Consciousness, the new World Civilization, and Group Initiation— take initiations as a kingdom and move into the Cave to become the Planetary Center of Synthesis. As Earth takes initiation, it will become a Solar Center of Synthesis, and as the Solar Life takes initiation it will become a Cosmic Center of Synthesis. That is why each of us, humanity, and the planetary life have been through so much, so that this dark star would, in the end, have so very much to give.

(Quinn closed his eyes and bowed his head, holding a radiant indigo-white cone of light —down, out, and up. The room remained absolutely still and silent, but for the slow breath of the audience.) ...

Quinn: "Prepare for meditation."

---

[27] Glen: This may be related to D.K.s remarks on that which lies behind the "three divine aspects" on p. 258 of *The Rays and The Initiations*, by Alice A. Bailey.

Closing Meditation

Quinn: "As a group, move upward via a line of indigo-white light, through the group crown center, through the Wisdom, to periphery of the Ashram of Synthesis.

"As the group in the periphery, invoke the purpose of the Ashram downward, and sound that purpose in the mental instrument by audibly sounding the OM.

"As the group, sound that purpose in the astral instrument by audibly sounding the OM.

"As the group, sound that purpose in the physical-etheric instrument by audibly sounding the OM.

"As the group, radiate that purpose outward to humanity by audibly sounding the OM.

"As the group, align humanity upward, via a line of indigo-white light, directly toward that purpose, and audibly sound the OM.

"Leaving the alignment in place, slowly relax the attention and return to your normal focus.

The group remained still and silent for some time, then finally stirred. I turned off the recorder and scooped up our things.

Quinn stood and bowed to the group, with palms together in front of his forehead, and said, "Namaste."

The group quietly echoed, "Namaste", and we departed, into the night.

Chapter 4

Afterword

Chantel lit our way, gliding before us, down the winding stair and out. Quinn paused outside, on the edge of the glow from the porch light, took a deep breath, and relaxed his alignment. The indigo-white glow faded along with its E-Sharp vibration, leaving his normal tone and color —a bit washed-out from exertion, but nothing more.

Then we stepped into the shadows and headed for the 'Cruiser. When we were inside, with the motor running, Quinn aligned with the 'Deva of Freeways' as he called it, and we drove away.

He waited until we'd merged onto the 405, and then asked, "What did you see?"

"They were clearer this time, less churned up. The tummy area—"

"Solar plexus?"

"Um, yes. The solar plexus was much calmer, and quieter. They moved up with the alignment much more quickly, before the opening med ended. As a group they held the note throughout the workshop, and it was clearer, sharper, and louder."

Quinn nodded, and said, "Good, good. That's the way 'Synthesis Through Chaos' works. Polarization, with dissonance and disagreement in the beginning, but we reached a degree of union and agreement by the end. Only four weeks, but it was a good start, and they did a very good job of invoking the Wisdom. Not many groups could have brought through that much so quickly.

"When you take up your function, your work will be similar, but of course with music and song rather than speech. So I want you to do the same kind of observing during the new course starting next week. It's a lot longer, so you'll have much more opportunity to observe what goes on, and I'll want written reports of each of those lessons as well.

"Now, it's late and you're tired. Why don't you ask Chantel to sing you to sleep?"

"OK."

Chantel called on a few friends, and I slept among a choir of angels until we reached home.

Bibliography

Bailey, Alice A., Lucis Publishing Company, New York, NY
  A Treatise on White Magic, 1934
  Discipleship in The New Age, Vol. I, 1944
  Discipleship in The New Age, Vol. II, 1955
  Externalization of the Hierarchy, The, 1957
  From Intellect to Intuition, 1932
  Glamour, A World Problem, 1950
  Rays and The Initiations, The, 1960

Cedercrans, Lucille, Wisdom Impressions Publishers, Whittier, CA
  Applied Wisdom, (2005)
  Ashramic Projections, 2004
  Creative Thinking, 2001
  Disciple and Economy, The, 2002
  Leadership Training, 2003
  Nature of The Soul, The, 1993
  Soul and Its Instrument, The, 1995

Knape, Glen, Preparation Press, Whittier, CA
  Raising the Queen of Heaven, 2005

For further information on the above works see:
  http://www.lucistrust.org/lucispub/
  http://www.wisdomimpressions.com/
  http://www.preparationpress.com/

The Magic of Consciousness – Workshops